First published in 2014 by Motorbooks, a member of Quarto Publishing Group USA Inc.,
400 First Avenue North, Suite 400, Minneapolis, MN 55401 USA

Motorbooks titles are also available at discounts in bulk quantity for industrial or sales-
promotional use. For details write to Special Sales Manager at Quarto Publishing Group USA Inc.,
400 First Avenue North, Suite 400, Minneapolis, MN 55401 USA.

To find out more about our books, visit us online at www.motorbooks.com.

ISBN-13: 978-0-7603-4552-8

Editors: Madeleine Vasaly, Jordan Wiklund
Design Manager: James Kegley
Designer: Simon Larkin

Printed in China

10 9 8 7 6 5 4 3 2

# DODGE
## 100 YEARS

*motorbooks*

# CONTENTS

# CHAPTER 1

# THE DODGE STORY BEGINS

Although John (left) was nearly four years older than Horace (right), their relationship was so close the pair could have been twins.

"I am tired of being carried around in Henry Ford's vest pocket."–John Francis Dodge, 1913.

That simple sentiment launched a car company. John and his brother, Horace Elgin Dodge, were Detroit machinists who, by 1913, had been for the better part of a decade supplying Henry Ford with most of the components used in building his cars.

The vest pocket imagery speaks not only to the close relationship that the Dodge brothers enjoyed with Ford, but also to the very essence of who these two men were, what they meant to each other, and just how huge their eventual impact on the auto industry would be.

It Speaks for Itself

DODGE BROTHERS, DETROIT

## FROM MACHINISTS TO MANUFACTURERS

At the turn of the 20th century, watches were typically found in vest pockets. And a pocket watch is a perfect metaphor for the Dodge brothers. They worked like a precision instrument, their two talents meshing seamlessly in clockwork fashion. John, the elder, was the visionary, handling the business end of things, while Horace was the mechanical genius who knew how to keep the enterprise ticking.

The mainspring was their humble upbringing. John was born October 25, 1864, followed by Horace about two and a half years later, on May 28, 1868. Born into a family of machinists—their father, Daniel, and two uncles practiced the trade—the pair grew up in southwest Michigan in the small town of Niles, before their father moved the family first to Battle Creek and then Port Huron before settling in Detroit in 1886.

The brothers worked at Murphy Boiler Works in Detroit doing rough machining work for six years before finding new jobs across the Detroit River in Windsor, Ontario, at the Dominion Typograph Company, where they added precision machining to their repertoire.

In 1896, after Horace invented and won a patent for a new kind of bicycle wheel bearing, the brothers struck out on their own. They started a Canadian bicycle company with Harold Evans, who they had met while employed by Dominion. The Evans & Dodge Bicycle venture lasted just four years—the Dodge duo sold their shares in 1900, taking their expertise back to Detroit where they established a machine shop.

Above: Like the car itself, the first advertisement was an exercise in simplicity. It showed the product, a list of general specifications, and the headline, "It Speaks for Itself."

Below: Guy Ameel, superintendent of final assembly, drives Horace (left) and John Dodge around Detroit in their first car, *Old Betsy*.

The Dodge Main assembly in 1916 adopted the moving assembly line pioneered by Henry Ford at his nearby Highland Park plant. Inset: Cars await shipment from Dodge Main. Dodge Brothers used steel bodies and enamel paint that could be cured in ovens, significantly shortening the time it took to produce cars.

A year later, they landed a contract to supply Ransom Eli Olds and his Olds Motor Works with engines for the famed Curved Dash. It was their first foray into the burgeoning automotive industry, and the Dodge Brothers machine shop was located a few blocks north of the OMW factory, which was on the Detroit River. The Olds site is now a parking lot in the shadow of General Motors' Renaissance Center headquarters.

A devastating fire in 1901 destroyed much of the OMW factory and, in turn, created the opportunity for more work for Dodge Brothers—the company was contracted to supply more than 2,000 transmissions to Oldsmobile.

Meanwhile, Henry Ford, after failing twice to start a car company, turned to Dodge Brothers to supply a wide range of components for his original Model A. Ford's third run at launching a car company proved to be the charm, thanks in no small part to Dodge Brothers. In fact, so successful was Dodge Brothers that the company supplied virtually complete chassis to Ford—Ford only needed to add a body and wheels to finish cars.

The relationship grew as Dodge churned out a generation of Ford vehicles, including the Model C and Model F, although Ford's Model B (which contained some Dodge content) relied on other companies for parts as a way for Ford to retain some leverage over its main supplier.

Still, in the rough-and-tumble early days of the auto industry, it was hardly smooth sailing. Due to Ford's low capitalization when it was incorporated, payments to Dodge Brothers were slow. But even this dark cloud had a silver lining that would turn to gold for Dodge. To settle some bookkeeping, Dodge Brothers wrote off $7,000 in overdue payments and took a $3,000 credit in exchange for a 10 percent share of Ford Motor Co. in 1903. It turned out to be the deal of the still-young century.

Not only did the Dodge Brothers profit handsomely over the next ten years from its exclusive supply contract with Ford, their holdings in Ford paid millions in dividends. Getting those dividends from the notoriously tight-fisted Henry Ford, however, proved difficult. The Dodge brothers joined a 1916 lawsuit brought by malcontent shareholders, forcing Ford to share its cash hoard. The Dodges finally sold their 10 percent stake in 1919 for $25 million.

The decade-long relationship with Ford (along with the money earned from fellow industry pioneers) allowed Dodge Brothers to expand, building a larger machine shop around the corner from their original shop, followed by a much larger factory in Hamtramck in 1910. Hamtramck

Above: One of Dodge's selling points was that the style of the car didn't change significantly from year to year, although there were constant improvements to the mechanicals. This 1921 model is nearly identical to the first cars.

Below: Dodge Main was one of the most advanced automobile factories of its time, as evidenced by the huge presses used to stamp out body parts.

was a Polish enclave located just a few miles from downtown Detroit and not far from Ford's new assembly plant in Highland Park. Dodge Brothers' new factory would later be known as Dodge Main, and proved to be the ideal launching pad for their first car.

What drove Dodge Brothers to build its own car isn't particularly clear-cut. Historian Richard Crabb maintains that it was a desire by the brothers to build a better car than Henry Ford, fueled in part by the automaker's refusal to incorporate product improvements suggested by his erstwhile suppliers.

Charles Hyde's authoritative work, *The Dodge Brothers: The Men, The Motorcars, The Legacy*, paints a slightly different picture. According to Theodore MacManus, who ran an ad agency that had Dodge as a client, the brothers met with their attorney Howard B. Bloomer, who asked them why they didn't consider building their own car. John Dodge is said to have been content with the Ford business and the dividend income, and didn't want to have the hassle of retailing cars to the public. But Bloomer advised them that their total dependence on Ford could be their undoing. The next day, John and Horace met again with Bloomer and agreed with his assessment.

By August 1913, John Dodge was publicly quoted as saying that he and his brother had been making plans to build their own car and had begun buying property to expand their Hamtramck plant. "Our business has grown too big to be dependent upon anyone else and we have decided to go into the manufacture of automobiles for ourselves," he told the press. In July, he had notified Henry Ford that Dodge would cease all work for him in 12 months' time.

As the work for Ford wound down, Horace Dodge shifted into high gear in developing the new car. Helping him was Frederick J. Haynes, whom the brothers had first met back in their Evans & Dodge Bicycle days. Haynes came to Detroit from the H. H. Franklin auto company in Syracuse,

Above: This electric sign for the Dodge Brothers plant was erected in 1915. The huge factory predates the first Dodge car by four years, having been built in 1910 to supply parts and chassis to Ford.

Below: The Dodge Main assembly plant was the first to have its own test track, where cars were given a shakedown drive after coming off the line.

New York, and proved instrumental in helping to transition the plant from making components to building complete automobiles.

The first car, dubbed "Old Betsy," rolled out of the plant on November 14. It was driven around Detroit with Horace and John Dodge in the rear and Guy Ameel, superintendent of production, behind the wheel.

While purported to be the first Dodge car off the assembly line, the press previewed "Old Betsy" before the roll-out ceremony where they learned that she was, in fact, a development car. This canny use of the press and advertising was key to the Dodge brothers in not only building demand for the car, but also attracting the dealer network they needed to launch and sustain the business.

Dodge's first dealer was John H. Cheek of Nashville, Tennessee. The son of Joel Cheek, who founded Maxwell House coffee, Cheek's father urged him to travel to Detroit to talk to the Dodge brothers. Cheek, who sold Chevrolet and REO cars through his Cumberland Motors, won the franchise and sold the first retail unit on December 22, 1914, and later gave up the Chevy business. When questioned by John Dodge about his high initial order of cars, Cheek responded, "If you don't shoot for the moon, you will never hit it." Chief among Cheek's later customers was famous World War I hero, Sergeant Alvin York—Check not only sold York his first car, but taught him how to drive.

Above: The Dodge Brothers logo, as shown in this 1918 sample, features intertwined letters, which serves to only underscore the close relationship between John and Horace.

Below: The wooden test track outside the plant was eventually torn down to make way for more buildings on the sprawling Doge Main factory site.

DODGE BROTHERS 4-DOOR SEDAN

**DODGE BROTHERS**
**BUSINESS CAR**

A car the business man can depend upon
for steady, everyday, low-cost service

Designed by Dodge Brothers to pay its way.

The haulage cost is unusually low

**DODGE BROTHERS, DETROIT**

Above: By the 1920s, the closed 4-door sedan became the volume leader in overall production numbers for Dodge. Inset: This 1918 ad for Dodge Brothers business cars shows the panel-side commercial vehicle, which was essentially a van body mounted on a standard car chassis.

John and Horace Dodge were the antithesis of Henry Ford, who is best described as ascetical in many ways. He didn't drink or smoke. The behaviors of the Dodge brothers, however, having grown up on the shop floor, were closer to the men they employed. Both loved to entertain and be entertained, and both greatly enjoyed their wealth. They lived in lavish homes, and Horace in particular was fond of powerboats. These divergent lifestyles were also reflected in the cars they built.

## BUILDING A BETTER CAR

Like the Model T, the first Dodge automobile could be had in any color as long as it was black. Its exterior styling did not change significantly for more than seven years, but it did evolve—more than can be said of the Model T, which remained unchanged until production ceased in 1927.

The Dodge differed in that it was a mid-priced car retailing at $785 vs. $490 for the Model T. It rode on a 110-inch wheelbase and was powered by a 35 bhp engine, compared to the T's output of 20 bhp. The Dodge was technically superior in other ways as well: it was the first production car to use a steel body and chassis (virtually all cars had wooden frames); it had a more sophisticated sliding gear transmission than the simpler planetary gear setup of the T; and it was the first car to use a 12-volt electrical system instead of 6-volt. And electric starting was standard, whereas the Model T offered that feature as an option over the standard hand crank.

While Ford used mass production to lower the cost of his cars year after year (by 1926, a Model T Roadster cost a mere $260), the Dodge approach was to continually upgrade the product mechanically while keeping the price fixed in the middle of the market.

The combination of styling, continual product improvements, and above all, durability—the cars gained tremendous credibility for their use by the U.S. Army in its 1916 Mexican campaign and World War I—burnished Dodge's reputation. Production ramped up, growing from just 43,033 in 1915 to 141,000 in 1920, putting Dodge solidly in second place behind Ford.

The Dodge lineup was the model of simplicity: an open 4-door touring car and open 2-seat roadster. By 1917, the wheelbase had been lengthened by 4 inches to 114 inches, but the car's design didn't appreciably change. Closed cars were offered in a coupe and a center-door sedan— this 5-passenger model had one door on each side in the center of the body, a style that didn't appeal to many buyers. The price of the closed car rose to $1,285.

Dodge began its long history of building commercial vehicles when it added a so-called screen-side business car—essentially a pickup truck version of the touring car with screened sides and a roof over the load floor. A panel version was soon offered, as well as a taxi.

This particular model featured a single door on each side to provide access to both the front and rear passenger compartment. It proved to be unpopular and was soon replaced by a conventional 4-door model.

By 1919, the model range had grown again with the addition of a conventional 4-door closed sedan and a 2-door, 5-window closed coupe. Prices ranged from $1,085 for the touring car and roadster to $1,750 for the closed coupe and sedan.

## THE DEMISE OF JOHN AND HORACE

While 1920 was a banner year for sales, it also marked a time of tragedy. During a January trip to the New York Auto Show, both John and Horace came down with influenza, which developed into pneumonia. Though Horace was originally harder hit, he eventually recovered. John, however, became critically ill, slipped into a coma, and died January 14, 1920. He was 55 years old.

Horace, still ill, but recovering, was unable to travel home to Detroit for the funeral. Following the death of his brother, he became inconsolable.

"The passing of my dear brother, Mr. John F. Dodge, is to me, personally [sic], a loss so great that I hesitate to look forward to the years without his companionship, our lives having been, as you all know, practically inseparable since our childhood," he wrote in a letter explaining his absence from company functions, including a celebration marking the production of the 500,000th Dodge in July, 1920.

Although he became president of the company in the wake of his brother's death, Horace began reorganizing the company to ensure that its legacy lived on by making Frederick Haynes a vice president. Neither Horace nor John's children showed significant interest in the business, and Horace wanted to ensure that New York investment banks would stay away from Dodge.

Above: This is one of the first Dodge Brothers logos. It dates back to the start of the car company in 1914, and the intertwined *D* and *B* became a recurring theme throughout the Dodge Brothers era.

Below: Available only in black, this roadster looks very similar to the Ford Model T. One significant difference is that Dodge offered such standard amenities as an electric starter.

Horace Dodge spent most of his time at his home in Palm Beach, Florida, returning only sporadically to Detroit to manage the business and his affairs. Later that year, he had a relapse and was bedridden for a period before returning to Florida, where he died on December 10, 1920. While some reports listed complications from influenza and pneumonia as the cause of death, the official report listed cirrhosis. He was 52 years old, and the Dodge brothers were no more.

Following Horace's death, ownership passed to the brothers' widows—Matilda Rausch Dodge, John's third wife, and Anna Thomson Dodge. Haynes was promoted to president, and Howard Bloomer, the attorney who advised Dodge to build its own car, was elected chairman.

Haynes stuck to the formula that had made Dodge Brothers a success—minimal cosmetic changes while making significant improvements to the product. In 1923, the company introduced a business coupe that was the industry's first all-steel closed car, followed that fall by an all-steel 4-door sedan.

Other new features added during this period included heaters, semi-floating rear axles, and engine upgrades to the 4-cylinder powerplant that had been unchanged since 1914. The cars' wheelbases grew to 116 inches without altering the basic look of the exterior design. The lack of styling changes became an advertising slogan in 1924: "Constantly Changed—No Yearly Models."

On the commercial side, Dodge continued to build the screen-side and panel van versions of its basic car, but Haynes also was also the driving force behind the eventual acquisition of

Above: One of the advantages enjoyed by Dodge Brothers was the ability to forge many of its components in-house. Here you see the vats used to cool the components as they come out of the forge—those that pass inspection are put into the carts, while the rejects are placed in a box next to the vat.

Inset: The entrance to the office building at Dodge Main is as unassuming as the Dodge Brothers themselves.

Horace Dodge        John Dodge

Graham Brothers, a maker of commercial vehicles—a move that would mark the beginning of Dodge's long history of truck leadership. Originally, the agreement was for Dodge to simply supply engines and transmission to Graham Brothers, but the parts and distribution relationship laid the foundation for Dodge to purchase Graham in 1925.

By January 1925, Matilda Rausch and Anna Thomson Dodge were ready to sell. They received over a dozen offers, but the number quickly whittled down to two—one from J. P. Morgan on behalf of General Motors for $124 million cash, or $90 million cash and $50 million in notes; Dillon, Read & Co., a New York investment bank, offered $146 million cash. The widows accepted the latter offer. Dodge was now controlled by outside financial interests, but for Walter Chrysler, it was the opportunity he had been waiting for.

Below: At the Dodge Main plant, this courtesy room featured a chassis as well as components, which can be seen on a display board in the background. The early-model Dodge shown here has a 4-cylinder engine and mechanical brakes.

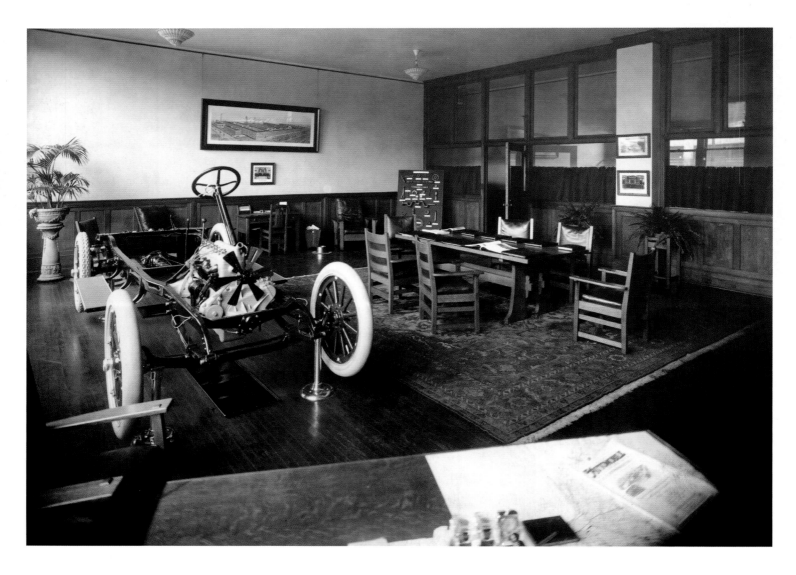

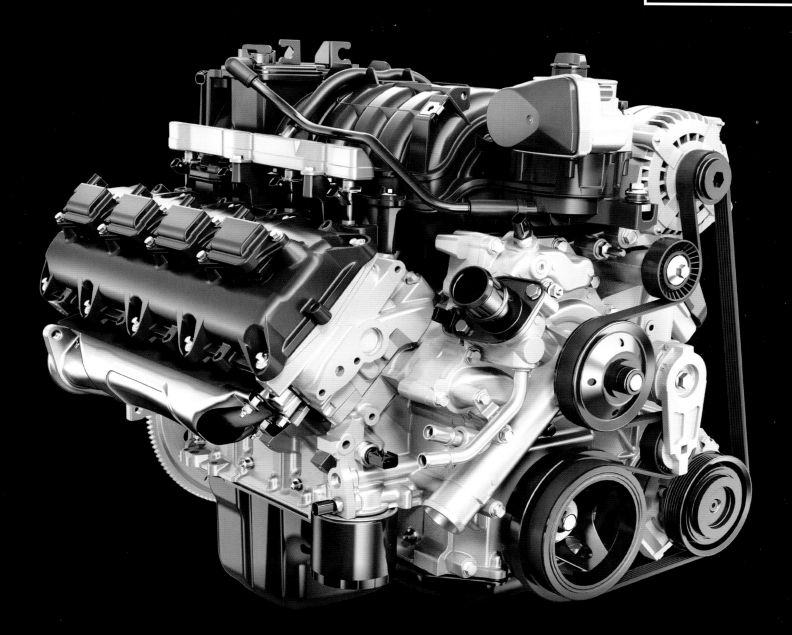

# CHAPTER 2

# TECHNOLOGY IN MOTION

One of the features of the 5.7-liter HEMI® V-8 engine is its Multi Displacement System (MDS), which allowed the engine to operate on just four cylinders at cruising speed to save fuel.

**The first car produced by the Dodge Brothers seems crude by today's standards.**

It was an open car, with no power options except for the electric starter. It didn't have a radio, heater, or even side glass unless you ordered the optional winter top, which cost an extra $165 over the base price of $795.

But that first car must be viewed in context. In 1914, it had been just 11 years since the Wright Brothers first flew a plane at Kitty Hawk. Most travel was primarily by train. There were no interstate highways. In fact, gasoline-powered cars still faced competition from steam and electric vehicles.

While the Model T is generally credited with putting America on wheels, a case can be made that the technological advancements incorporated in the first Dodge automobile laid the foundation for the industry to have a lasting impact on society. The dependability, high quality,

Right: The technical advancements in the Dodge product lineup were designed not only for dependability, but also for ease of use, as this ad shows in touting the semiautomatic transmission, hydraulic brakes, and vibration-damping engine mounts.

Below: In 1928, the introduction of the Dodge Victory Six was an automotive innovation; for the first time, the body was welded to the chassis. This particular model is shown on a stand for the Budd Company, which developed the process.

# DODGE
## *with* Floating Power

*Automatic Clutch, Silent Gear Selector and Free Wheeling*

*The New Eight Coupe $1115*
*(Special equipment extra)*

*FLASHING ACTION without sound or tremor —*
*pedal-free gear shifting — a new motoring experience*

A RIDE that's as silent, as effortless, as breathlessly thrilling as coasting down a snow-clad hillside . . . that's the sensation you get in the new Dodge Six and Eight.

*Floating Power,* as applied to the lively Dodge six- and eight-cylinder engines, gives a flow of performance you can neither hear nor feel.

You can forget the clutch pedal . . . the Dodge Automatic Clutch, the Silent Gear Selector and the separate Free Wheeling unit combine to make gear-shifting merely a matter of moving a lever that responds like

silent magic to the driver's lightest touch.

Weatherproof Hydraulic Brakes with new-type drums give you effortless speed control. Silent Mono-Piece Steel Bodies, tremendously strong Bridge-Type Double-Drop Frames and a very low center of gravity give a degree of steadiness and roadability

*Hydraulic Brakes . Silent Second*
*Gear . Low Center of Gravity*
*Double-Drop Bridge - Type Frame*
*Mono-Piece Steel Bodies . . . .*

that makes an all-day trip as fatigue-free as a five-minute ride.

Nothing in the world can quite prepare you for the joy you will find in driving these cars. Just get behind the wheel. Then try to justify buying any car that offers less.

NEW LOW PRICES

NEW DODGE SIX . . . . . . . $795 to $845
NEW DODGE EIGHT . . . . . $1115 to $1145

*F. O. B. Detroit. Low delivered prices. Convenient terms. Five wire or demountable wood wheels, no extra cost. Duplate safety plate glass at new low price. Automatic Clutch only $8 additional on all Sixes. Closed models factory-wired for Philco-Transitone.*

# DODGE DEPENDABILITY

and continual improvements to gasoline-powered cars not only helped Dodge grow, but also settled the debate over what kind of technology would be used for the next 100 years, from gasoline engines to all-steel bodies.

In its layout, the first Dodge was fairly typical. Like most cars of the era, it had a four-stroke, 4-cylinder engine which drove the rear wheels. But for its price, it also had features that were more likely found on cars costing hundreds or even thousands more, like the sliding gear transmission; the pressurized fuel system at a time when some cars had hand pumps to charge the tank; a standard electric starter instead of a hand crank; and a 12-volt electrical system for the spark plugs, lights, and electric horn.

Above: This 1930 Dodge DD was equipped with a 60-horsepower, 190-cubic-inch inline 6-cylinder engine. Note that the brakes are hydraulic, a feature that set the $835 Dodge apart from others in its class.

## DODGES' BEST BUDD

The most significant aspect of the first Dodge car was its industry-first all-steel construction. Perhaps it was the Dodges' background as machinists working with metal that led them to the conclusion that a steel body would be superior to the wood or wood/metal bodies employed by other manufacturers.

This led to a relationship between Dodge Brothers and Edward G. Budd Manufacturing, based in Philadelphia. Edward Budd had gotten his start producing pressed steel pedestals for railroad car seats as well as sheet steel walls and bodies for Pullman cars at Hale & Kilburn. While that company made an all-steel body for Hupmobile in 1912 on the Model 32, only a limited number were built, and before the year was out, the company had returned to the more conventional steel-over-wood body construction.

Above: By 1938, Dodge adopted a completely steel body with a full-steel roof panel to replace the conventional wood-and-fabric insert that had been standard industry practice.

Right: The introduction of the Red Ram V-8 engine in 1953 marked the return of an engine with more than six cylinders after a long absence. The 241-cubic-inch engine made 140 horsepower.

It's like money in the bank! Even when you're not using it, nice to know it's there . . . this surge of

extra **Power**

CORONET V-EIGHT CLUB COUPE

**New-All New**

**'53 Dodge**

In the new 140-h.p. Red Ram V-Eight engine, Dodge engineers have provided you with a magnificent reserve of acceleration and performance. You take to the highway with greater confidence, greater safety.

And with this surging Red Ram power, you enjoy nimble change-of-pace of new Gyro-Torque Drive.

A new road-hugging, curve-holding ride.

A new sense of driving mastery.

If your active life demands an Action Car . . . this sleek, trim Dodge is for you. "Road Test" it . . . soon.

Specifications and equipment subject to change without notice.

In the meantime, Budd had left the company and formed his own, and in 1914, received a contract from Dodge to build 5,000 all-steel bodies for their new car as well as fenders. This business enabled Budd to get his newly patented all-steel welded auto body into regular production.

The all-steel body, which was attached to the car's steel frame, had particular advantages in the paint process, where it was covered with enamel and baked in an oven to dry as opposed to the wood/metal bodies, which couldn't be heat-treated because of warpage. Instead, as many as 20 coats were hand-applied and rubbed out, a process that could take as long as two weeks. The all-metal bodies could be primed and painted in less than half the time.

Budd continued to work with Dodge and in 1928 created the first car to use unit-body construction, a process where the steel body and frame were welded together to create a single monocoque. While the 1934 Chrysler Airflow is often cited as the first unit-body car in the industry, Dodge actually preceded it by six years. Although Dodge used steel bodies since its inception, the roof panel (per industry practice) was still made of wood and fabric. In 1937, full- steel roof panels were incorporated.

While Chrysler has long had a reputation for a being an engineering-driven company, some of that reputation can be traced back to Dodge Brothers. When Walter P. Chrysler acquired the firm in 1928, one of the first ad campaigns was titled, "What Chrysler engineers have found out about Dodge Brothers." The campaign extolled the technical expertise of its newest division, and as a result, Chrysler technical firsts would also be Dodge technical firsts.

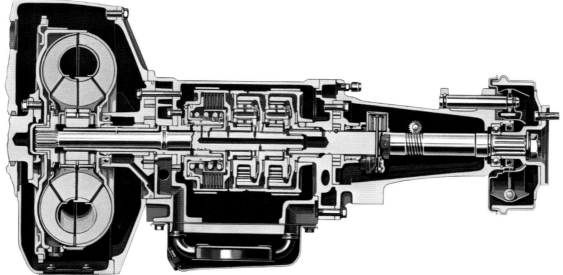

Top: Another advancement that helped both ride and handling was the use of an independent front suspension. The A-arms are visible in this top-down view.

Above: Dodge introduced pushbuttons on the 1956 models—the PowerFlite transmission has just four buttons—Neutral, Reverse, Drive, and Low. The car was started in neutral, and reverse had a feature that automatically shifted into neutral if the vehicle speed exceeded 10 miles per hour.

Left: Using a 2-speed planetary gear set, the PowerFlite automatic transmission was introduced on Dodge cars in 1954 and featured what would become the standard gear selection sequence of PRNDL.

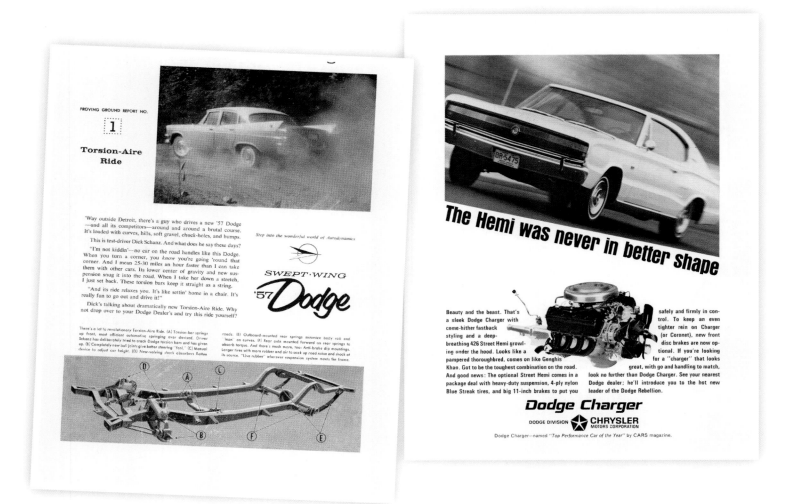

Above: In 1957, Dodge introduced a torsion bar suspension. In this ad, which explains the advantages of the TorsionAire suspension, the torsion bars can be seen linking the control arms to the chassis ahead of the front axle.

Right: This ad announces the introduction of the 426 Street HEMI engine as a customer option, opening the door for the race version of the powerplant to return to NASCAR competition.

The Dodge way of always improving the technical competency of the product began to expand beyond making the car more powerful, efficient, and durable. Now, these changes would be focused on making the car ride better and drive easier.

The all-steel bodies provided a rigid platform, and throughout the 1920s, the cars evolved from largely open affairs to closed coupes and sedans with creature comforts like heaters.

By the 1930s, high on the improvements list was reducing noise, vibration, and harshness (NVH). Dodge adopted a new engine-mount system called Floating Power, which was first introduced on the Plymouth in 1931 and the Dodge in 1932. Floating Power used tuned front and rear engine mounts to reduce engine vibration. Other innovations, like helical-cut gears in the transmission, reduced whine, and in 1934, an independent front suspension called Floating Cushion smoothed out the car's ride.

In making the cars easier to drive, Dodge quickly added power hydraulic brakes and began to offer semi-automatic transmissions that used a fluid coupling to minimize the use of the clutch and gearshift. Drivers could now select either high or low range, and only use the clutch to shift between the two gears or when engaging reverse.

Fuel economy was a primary concern even then, and Dodge offered an overdrive gear (which reduced engine rpm at higher speeds) and freewheeling (which disengaged the drivetrain when coasting) for improved efficiency. Dodge marketed transmission under a variety of names including Gyro-Matic, Fluid-Matic, Fluidtorque, and Gyro-Torque.

Other advances during those prewar years included the introduction of automatic spark advance (it previously was controlled by a lever on the steering wheel), the use of roller bearings in the universal joints, and in 1940, sealed-beam headlamps.

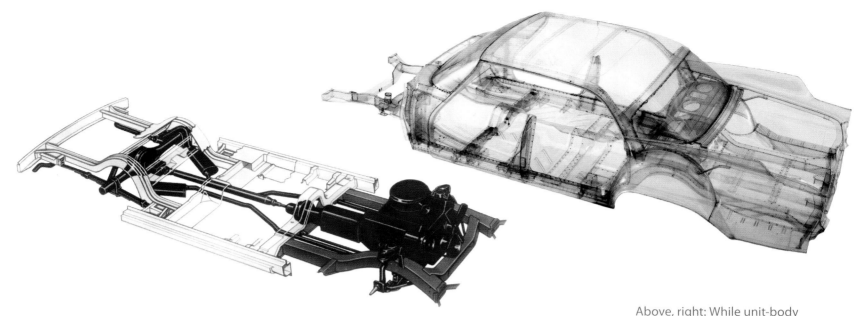

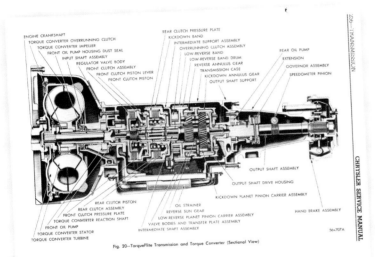

Fig. 20—TorqueFlite Transmission and Torque Converter (Sectional View)

Above, left: This cutaway of a 1960 Dodge Dart shows how the body is strengthened by using box sections to replace the traditional ladder frame.

Left: The next advance beyond the 2-speed PowerFlite transmission was the 3-speed TorqueFlite automatic. Introduced in 1956, the main body of this transmission became a mainstay in the Dodge lineup through the 1990s.

Above, right: While unit-body construction was not a new idea, the 1960 Dodge took it a step further in eliminating the chassis frame and incorporating those supports within the body shell itself, as can be seen in this cutaway drawing.

Below: The creation of a whole new class of vehicles with the 1984 Dodge Caravan was made possible by Dodge taking the lead in switching to compact front-drive platforms with transversely mounted engines.

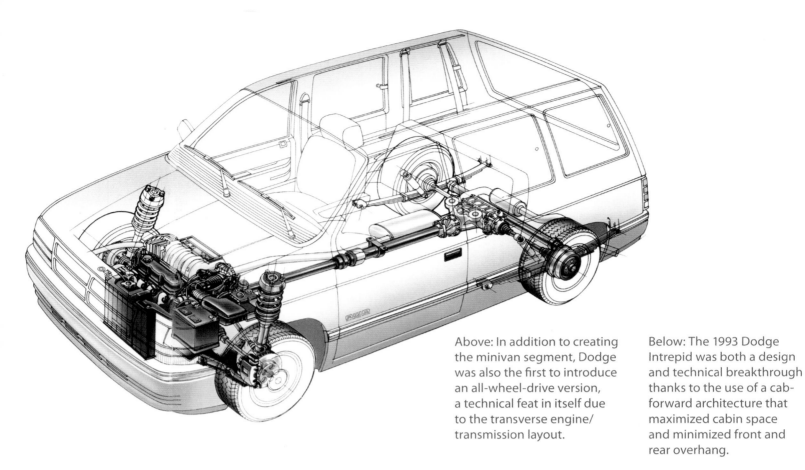

Above: In addition to creating the minivan segment, Dodge was also the first to introduce an all-wheel-drive version, a technical feat in itself due to the transverse engine/ transmission layout.

Below: The 1993 Dodge Intrepid was both a design and technical breakthrough thanks to the use of a cab-forward architecture that maximized cabin space and minimized front and rear overhang.

# TORSION BAR BREAKTHROUGH

After the war, the first all-new models came in 1949 and featured key-operated ignition and starter switches, waterproof ignition, resistor spark plugs, and a year later, 4-wheel self-energizing hydraulic disc brakes.

More comfort and convenience items were introduced in the 1950s, like electric window lifts (1954), pushbuttons on the 3-speed TorqueFlite automatic transmission and solid-state transistor radios (1956), swiveling front seats to ease egress (1959), and even an in-car record player. The record player used special records that played at 16 2/3 rpm, and later 45 rpm records, and electroluminescent faces on instruments (1960).

One of the best-known innovations from this era was the torsion bar front suspension. Although the concept was not new to the industry, when it was introduced in 1957, it represented the first time that a volume manufacturer had introduced the technology on a mid-price car. The setup employed conventional leaf-spring solid-axle rear suspensions, but up-front longitudinal bars that were anchored in a body crossmember and connected to the lower control arm of the front suspension. The twisting on this rod provided the spring action to counteract the up-and-down movement of the front wheels as they went over bumps. Torsion bars tended to provide better control because of their inherent stiffness over more traditional coil springs.

Called Torsion-Aire, this suspension had other advantages in that it was more compact, allowing for lower mounting of the engine. This in turn lowered the vehicle's center of gravity, which helped handling. Also, torsion bars proved to be easier to service, adjust, and replace than coil springs.

Torsion bar suspensions were used in this configuration until the 1978 introduction of the Dodge Aspen, which mounted the torsion bars transversely rather than longitudinally, a design that continued to until 1992 on the Dodge Diplomat.

One of the features of the 5.7-liter HEMI V-8 engine is its Multi Displacement System (MDS), which allowed the engine to operate on just four cylinders at cruising speed to save fuel.

Left: One of the big differences between the Intrepid and other front-drive cars in its class was the longitudinal mounting of the engine. This allowed for a lower hoodline and tighter turning radius.

Above: The 2014
Dodge Durango.

## ELECTRONIC EVOLUTION

The Muscle Car Era of the 1960s is viewed as a golden age—the cars were lean, mean, loud, and proud. The 1970s, on the other hand, are more or less the automotive dark ages, as two oil shocks, vehicle downsizing, and strict emission and fuel economy restrictions threw a wrench in the collective socket of car lovers everywhere. But in terms of technical innovations, the '70s were a time when Dodge and Chrysler made huge strides. This was especially true in the emerging field of on-board electronics.

Among these firsts were the use of electronic spark advance control (1976) and the Hall effect electronic distributor (1978). The '78 model year also marked the launch of the first American production car, the Dodge Omni, with front-wheel drive and a transversely mounted engine.

Dodge vehicles were among the first American cars to offer radial tires as standard equipment on all models in 1979, and for Big Gulp lovers everywhere, was the first to offer modern cupholders in 1983. That year also saw the advent of the talking car, with pre-recorded speaking messages and warnings.

The electronics revolution continues to this day with Dodge in the forefront of electronically controlled transmissions, a class-leading 8.4-inch touchscreen in the 2013 Dodge Dart and Uconnect Access via Mobile on the 2014 Dodge Durango, which allows owners to take their personal Internet radio playlists and stations with them on the road.

## THAT THING GOT A HEMI®? (PART 1)

While much has been done to make cars more dependable, comfortable, and easy-to-drive, the heart of every Dodge is its engine. And over the past century, the company has produced remarkable powerplants that are legendary in their own right. John and Horace Dodge started with relatively modest 4-cylinder power, but Dodge would go on to become known for HEMI V-8 engines and Slant Sixes before coming full circle back to a new generation of advanced 4-cylinder engines.

It was the 1953 introduction of the Red Ram V-8 engine that brought HEMI engine power to Dodge. At 241 cubic inches and making 140 horsepower, the Red Ram was the little brother to the 180-horsepower 331-cubic-inch HEMI engine introduced by Chrysler two years earlier. The hemispherical combustion chamber mixed the air and gasoline better, which enabled more complete burning of the fuel charge. It also improved the flow through the engine. The technology enhanced both power and fuel economy, and the HEMI engine's displacement and legend grew throughout the '50s and '60s.

In 1960, the Slant Six inline 6-cylinder engine was introduced. It was notable for its aluminum construction and its 30-degree offset of the bank from perpendicular, which allowed for better packaging. Because the cylinders were tilted to one side, the engine wasn't as tall as conventional inline sixes, and allowed for a lower hoodline favored by designers. The engineers liked it too, because the offset gave the car a lower center of gravity, which contributed to better handling. This 225-cubic-inch workhorse served in the Dodge lineup until 1984.

In 1981, Dodge returned to an in-house-built 4-cylinder engine, a 2.2-liter unit, introduced on the Omni. In addition to offering the 2.2-liter normally aspirated and turbo versions, a larger

Pentastar V-6 engines.

Left: The 5.7-liter HEMI V-8 engine returned to the Dodge lineup in 2005 with the introduction of the Magnum. This 2006 installation in HEMI Orange is on a Charger.

Above: Through its racing heritage, Dodge learned much about how aerodyanmics affects top speed. In the 1980s, it leveraged that know-how to boost fuel economy of its vehicles. The Dodge Shadow is one of many products that benefited from tests in the wind tunnel.

Right: In addition to continuing to offer advanced engines, Dodge has also built on its reputation for having class-leading automatic transmissions, including this new 8-speed unit.

2.5-liter variant was also developed. This engine family became a mainstay across the Dodge line, available in vehicles as diverse as the O24 Omni coupe up through the Grand Caravan minivan.

Dodge offered its first V-6 engine in 1988 (it earlier offered a 3.0-liter Mitsubishi produced V-6 engine) with an optional 3.3-liter pushrod unit in the Dynasty full-size sedan. That engine was later enlarged to 3.8 liters, and was also optional on top-line Dynasty models.

Soon, those engines were replaced with a new family of overhead cam V-6 engines displacing 2.7, 3.2, and 3.5 liters, respectively, and were offered in the Intrepid, which replaced the Dynasty as the largest Dodge in the range.

In the meantime, HEMI engine power, which had all but disappeared in the 1970s, returned, first in the 2003 Ram, and then in 2005 with the 5.7-liter V-8 engine in the Dodge Magnum, an engine later used in the Charger and Challenger. This engine was at the forefront of technology by offering MDS, a multiple displacement system that allowed the engine to run in 8-cylinder power or 4-cylinder economy modes.

In 2011, Dodge introduced the 305-horsepower 3.6-liter Pentastar V-6, an all-new engine that replaced the previous-generation V-6 powerplants.

Coming full circle over the 100-year history of Dodge, the two newest engines in the Dodge family are the 2.0-liter and 2.4-liter Tigershark 4-cylinder engines, which make a respective 160 and 184 horsepower, a far cry from Dodge Brothers' first inline-4 engine which displaced 3.5 liters and made just 35 horsepower. Technology has changed, but the continuing desire to improve the product has remained a constant at Dodge.

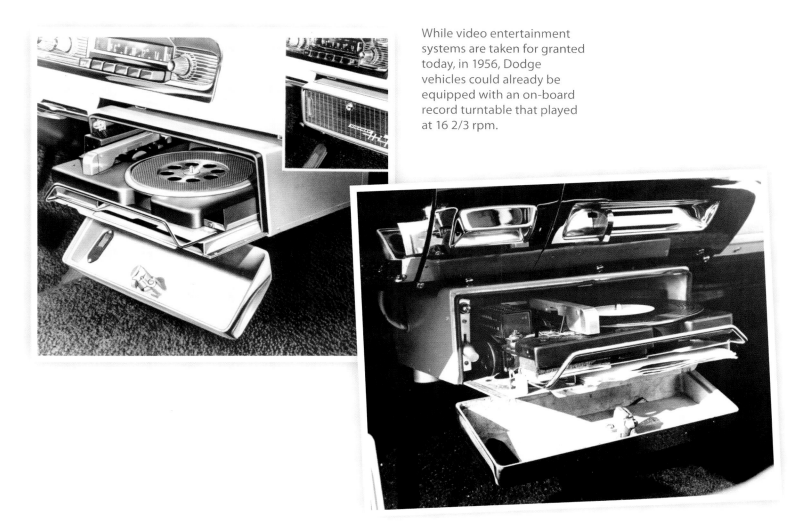

While video entertainment systems are taken for granted today, in 1956, Dodge vehicles could already be equipped with an on-board record turntable that played at 16 2/3 rpm.

# WALTER P. CHRYSLER'S COUP

The Victory Six bridged the gap between the Fast Four entry-level model and the more expensive and larger Senior Six.

The sale of Dodge Brothers to Dillon, Read & Co. on April 4, 1925, opened a brief chapter in the company's history where much of the previous decade's work to make Dodge successful unraveled.

Frederick J. Haynes, handpicked by Horace to lead Dodge into the future, was kicked upstairs into the largely ceremonial position as board chairman. He eventually left the company and worked at Durant Motors (founded by William "Billy" Durant after his ouster from the General Motors he created) before returning to Franklin.

The New York investment bankers brought in their own managers. They named 39-year-old Edward G. Wilmer, an attorney and turnaround specialist, as president. Wilmer joined Dodge from Goodyear Tire & Rubber, where he led that company back to profitability.

Wilmer decided that Dodge Brothers had been too conservative and launched a massive product onslaught for the late 1920s, introducing a new range of more expensive 6-cylinder cars. The first car Wilmer showcased was the Senior Six line, introduced in May 1927, priced from $1,495 for the 2-door. Meanwhile, the 4-cylinder line was also reworked and introduced that summer, followed in January 1928 by the Victory Six, priced between the so-called Fast Four and the Senior Six.

Normally, all new products introduced over such a short period of time would generate sales activity. The strategy of moving Dodge into a higher price bracket, however, combined with the short life of the Fast Four only caused confusion. Buyers looking for traditional Dodge values were disappointed, and sales fell.

While the Senior Six—the intended replacement of the Fast Four—had such technically advanced features as hydraulic brakes, the pricier car seemed at odds with the basic Dodge premise of offering solid, dependable transportation at an affordable price.

Below, left: During the brief Dillon, Read era, a revised version of the standard Dodge called the Fast Four was introduced in 1928, but it lasted barely a year on the market. This aviation-themed ad shows how the new management was looking to push the brand upmarket.

Below, right: The Senior Six line, which was priced at $1,495, was introduced in May 1927. Built at the Lynch Road plant, it used a Continental engine and a composite steel and wood body, unlike the all-steel cars coming from Dodge Main.

Still, the Victory Six line of cars and the Standard Six that replaced the Fast Four were more successful thanks to the fact that they were still being built at Dodge Main and incorporated the steady advancements that had become the company's way of doing business since its founding.

The Victory and Standard models used engines built by Dodge and the steel body and chassis construction developed by Budd Company continued with yet another important innovation. The practice at the time was to build a car with the body riding on the frame or chassis, called body-on-frame construction. Dodge practiced this technique, but also implemented a new way using both inner and outer body construction, allowing the seats, floor, and body panels to attach directly to the chassis to form a single unit, which also had the benefit of a lower ride height. Though little known, this development precedes the first generally recognized use of the technology, which ironically was the 1934 Chrysler Airflow.

Despite all these new products, Dodge Brothers production fell by nearly 40 percent in 1927, from 265,000 to 146,000 units. The declining sales and profitability convinced Dillon, Read & Co. that it needed to get the company into proper hands as soon as possible.

It was the moment Walter P. Chrysler was waiting for.

## BIRTH OF THE BIG THREE

**There couldn't have been a better savior for Dodge than Walter P. Chrysler, a machinist by trade in the mold of John and Horace.**

Born April 2, 1875, in Wamego, Kansas, Walter Percy Chrysler worked for a number of railroads throughout Kansas, Texas, and Iowa before moving to Pittsburgh. He was convinced to move to Detroit to work in the auto industry and was hired by Charles Nash to run production for Buick. Billy Durant subsequently appointed Chrysler to run the division. But it wasn't to be—Chrysler left Buick in 1919 in a dispute with Durant and landed at Willys-Overland where he was paid an unheard-of salary of $1 million per year.

Top: Seeking to reassure customers and dealers alike that the Dodge brand would not disappear, this ad bearing Walter P. Chrysler's signature touted a new lineup of vehicles for 1929 that became known as the Dodge Brothers Six.

Above: Part of the Dodge legacy of building comfortable and user-friendly cars is reflected in this 1934 ad that boasts of the car's independent front suspension.

Right: Even as late as 1932, the basic look of Dodge roadsters hadn't changed much over the years, although this particular model was one of the first to carry the Ram mascot.

Above: While Chrysler and DeSoto introduced their radical Airflow designs in 1934, the streamlining influence at Dodge was limited to the grille.

Left: Body styles continued to proliferate into the 1930s. This 1933 Dodge Westchester Suburban is one of the first woodies offered by the division, which ironically was best known for its all-steel bodies.

Right: The assembly line at Dodge Main reflects the continual improvements made to the plant over the years. By 1934, the factory was noticeably cleaner, while improvements like rollers in the floor automatically moved cars down the line.

Below: This exterior shot of Dodge Main shows the administration building and a smaller exhibition space right in front to showcase the division's products.

Nonetheless, Chrysler left Willys in 1921 after failing to gain control of the company. Soon, however, the same bankers he worked with who helped him take Willys-Overland from receivership helped him do the same with the Maxwell company, and over time (along with more help from additional parties), he purchased the majority of the struggling Maxwell stock and turned it into Chrysler Corp. in 1925.

By the time Dillon, Read & Co. was ready to exit Dodge, Chrysler—having decided to add two new brands in the entry-level Plymouth and mid-priced DeSoto to complement the flagship Chrysler range—was in need of additional factory space. While he first looked at Willys-Overland as a possible partner, he had his sights set on Dodge Brothers for its state-of-the-art Dodge Main plant as well as the additional capacity afforded by the new Lynch Road facilities. Chrysler also sought to benefit from the strong Dodge dealer network, which boasted more than 4,500 stores, bringing the total number of outlets for the merged company to about 9,000.

According to Walter Chrysler's autobiography, *Life of an American Workman*, Clarence Dillon approached him in April 1928 about the sale of Dodge. But Chrysler feigned disinterest since he had just announced the creation of DeSoto, which was priced to *rival* Dodge. After an initial back-and-forth, the two men began negotiation in earnest, renting adjoining suites at the Ritz-Carlton in New York and conducting a marathon five-day bargaining session. The key to the deal from Chrysler's perspective was to gain control with a stock swap that provided for a minimal cash outlay.

On May 29, the deal was submitted to the boards of Chrysler and Dodge, and the takeover became official on July 31, 1928.

## DODGE BROTHERS ONCE AGAIN

**Chrysler installed K. T. Keller, who had been his master mechanic at Buick, as head of Dodge. Keller was instrumental in integrating the Dodge works into Chrysler, and by 1935 Keller became Chrysler president.**

Because of Dodge's lackluster sales performance in 1927 and 1928, there was genuine concern that Chrysler would drop the Dodge Brothers nameplate in favor of DeSoto. But Chrysler moved quickly to dispel the rumors by moving ahead with product improvements for the Senior line, which included a larger body, increased wheelbase, and a more powerful engine. To underscore this commitment, Walter Chrysler insisted that the full Dodge Brothers nameplate be brought back. "Dodge Brothers Motor Cars will continue to bear the name they have borne so honorably, for fourteen years," Chrysler announced in an ad, further promising "Dodge Brothers dealers will continue to market them throughout the world."

And so, the Victory Six lineup was renamed the Dodge Brothers Six. That naming convention continued in 1930 when the division introduced its first 8-cylinder-powered car, which was called the Dodge Brothers Eight.

While Dodge Brothers had a stylish logo that featured intertwined letters of D and B signifying Dodge Brothers and interlocking Deltas (the symbol, often confused for the Star of David, featured contrasting colors, each one representing one of the brothers), Dodge never really had a mascot or hood ornament. It was left to Avard Fairbanks, who was on the faculty of the art school at the University of Michigan, to come

Above: Year-to-year model changes were minor in comparison to what would come in the 1950s. This '36 model features a slightly different grille than the '35.

Below: While Dodge avoided sharing the Airflow body style with Chrysler, streamlining influences could be seen by 1935, especially in the area of the grille cap and the rounded roofline. Even though it had a steel body, the roof panel was still made of wood and fabric.

Below: As part of its 25th anniversary, Dodge introduced its Luxury Liner model. 363 units were fitted with special bodies from Hayes. Dodge styling sported pontoon fenders and a split grille theme.

Bottom: With a new grille and pontoon-style front fenders, the Dodge Luxury Liner Deluxe was the last major redesign before World War II. When postwar production resumed, the same design was used with just minor trim changes.

up with a design to complement the mermaid he created for Plymouth and the leaping gazelle for the Imperial brand.

His favorite design was a ram's head, but reportedly Chrysler was dubious because a ram was just a male sheep. Supposedly Fairbanks persisted, saying the ram was the king of the trail, and that if you saw one coming, you'd think "dodge." Chrysler is said to have liked the idea, and that the ram iconography worked well with the one-word Dodge slogan: "Dependable."

During this initial period of the acquisition, Dodge was positioned above DeSoto and below Chrysler, with Plymouth as the entry-level car. By 1933, it was decided that Dodge would swap places with DeSoto, with the latter becoming the steppingstone to Chrysler, while Imperial represented the corporation's flagship line.

As part of this move, the Dodge division would no longer offer the 92-horsepower 232 cubic-inch straight eight, which had been sold for just four model years. From the 1934 model year until the advent of the HEMI V-8 engine in 1953, 6-cylinder engines powered all Dodge products.

The Dodge Eight, which had been based on a longer wheelbase than the 6-cylinder models, was replaced by a new 117-inch wheelbase DeLuxe Six in 1934. Prices changed dramatically— the most expensive Dodge in 1933 was the convertible sedan version of the Eight, which retailed for $1,365. A year later, the flagship DeLuxe Six in the same convertible sedan body style cost just $845.

This change in price class reflected the fact that Dodge was sharing more of its components with entry-level Plymouth, while DeSoto would partner with Chrysler for body stampings and mechanicals. The new order on the product ladder would have profound implications in the futures for both Dodge and DeSoto.

# AIRSTREAM TRUMPS AIRFLOW

In 1934, in the midst of the aerodynamics craze sweeping the worlds of transportation, architecture, and popular art, Chrysler brought out the Airflow. This streamlined range of cars shared among DeSoto, Chrysler, and Imperial featured a swept back radiator, rear wheel skirts, and rounded proportions. Though they look fantastic and retro today, at the time they failed to catch the public's fancy.

Dodge and Plymouth kept their more conservative lines, with only their grilles getting the streamlining treatment. A plan to move to the Airflow design for Dodge by 1935 was abandoned as a result of the unpopularity of the new design.

Instead, the 1935 models were fitted with waterfall grilles, rounded lines, and skirted wheels as part of the new "Airstream" look, which was a much more restrained take on the Airflow design. During this period, Dodge models became known for having a prow-like nose, pontoon-style fenders, and long rear decks on 2-door models.

Despite the Great Depression, Dodge sales continued to climb through the mid-1930s. From a low point of just 27,234 units produced in 1932, Dodge output peaked at 313,012 in 1937, a testament to its conservative approach to styling and affordable pricing.

Giving 1937 sales a boost was that year's product improvements. These upgrades to Dodge and the rest of the Chrysler divisions were implemented with an eye toward safety, including recessed dash knobs, curved-in door handles that promised not to snag coat sleeves, and padded front seat backs to protect the rear-seat passengers in sudden stops.

Above: This aerial view of the Dodge Main assembly plant shows a sprawling industrial complex that continued to grow as production was increased.

Below: The interlocking Deltas are still visible in this winged emblem from 1938.

Bottom: The badge for the 1938 Dodge features wings (a trend that started earlier in the 1930s). The interlocking Deltas in the middle of the badge were often mistaken for the Star of David.

To celebrate Dodge Brothers' 25th anniversary in 1939, Dodge introduced an all-new Luxury Liner with a new body in special and deluxe trim. It also marked the end of the Dodge Brothers interlocking triangles badge in favor of labeling the cars simply as Dodge.

In addition to these models, a limited-edition run of 1,000 cars with Hayes bodywork were also built for Chrysler, DeSoto and Dodge, of which Dodge received 363. It was the priciest car in the lineup, retailing at $1,055.

While the basic body design introduced in 1939 remained the same, trim levels and wheelbases continued to evolve. The standard wheelbase increased in 1940 from 117 to 119.5 inches. The I-6 engine, unchanged since 1934 in its 218 cubic inch displacement and 87 horsepower, benefited from a bump in output in 1941 to 91 horsepower, while in 1942 (the last year Dodge cars built until the end of World War II), the I-6 engine had a larger 230-cubic-inch engine making 105 horsepower.

The 1930s were significant in that the Dodge's identity, which was positioned squarely in the middle of the market, was firmly cemented. The reputation for durability and value would serve Dodge well throughout the war years, and set the tone for the second half of the 20th century.

During the streamlining craze of the 1930s, Chrysler released the radically styled Airflow in 1934. It was a shape shared by both Imperial and DeSoto. The look failed to catch on with buyers, and the more conservatively styled Dodge saw its market share increase.

# CHAPTER 4

THE NEW
TWO-DOOR SEDAN

## WOMEN LOVE TO DRIVE IT

Women choose the new Dodge Six with confidence because it bears the honored name of Dodge Brothers. They *drive* it with confidence, under all conditions of traffic and travel, because it handles and controls so simply and surely. It is easy for feminine hands to turn sharp corners with the Dodge steering gear—to flash nimbly around other automobiles on crowded streets—to park in spaces scarcely larger than the Dodge Six itself—easy for feminine feet to operate the clutch as well as to apply the "soft", sure-action internal-expanding 4-wheel hydraulic brakes. Above all, it is easy for *anyone* to own this charming car. Its first price is surprisingly moderate—its maintenance cost practically negligible—and its operation expense extremely low.

CONVENIENT TERMS

## NEW DODGE BROTHERS SIX

CHRYSLER MOTORS PRODUCT

# THE DODGE PROMISE

By the time Dodge Brothers launched its first car, marketing and advertising were already well-established means of selling products. And there were more than a fair share of practitioners who were willing to bend or stretch the truth in order to make a sale.

Not so with Dodge. The essence of the Dodge Brothers approach to building cars was elegant in its simplicity: build a high-quality and durable car that offered continual product improvements rather than offering cosmetic changes just for the sake of change itself.

The straightforward approach to selling Dodge vehicles can be seen in its advertising and marketing, which communicated in a simple and straightforward fashion the innate advantages of Dodge ownership In turn, the sales successes were tangible proof that the company was on the right track.

By stressing the ease of driving thanks to advancements such as hydraulic brakes, Dodge sought to broaden its appeal among women with ads targeted directly to them.

This simple, honest approach to selling cars can also be seen in the announcement of the company's birth. One of its first ads touts Dodge Brothers' abilities in producing auto components: "In a plant accustomed to heating and forging 300,000 pounds of steel a day—with every other operation on a scale of equal magnitude—Dodge Brothers are now manufacturing their own car. They are bringing to bear upon it everything that tends to produce value—extraordinary experience; immense production capacity; complete financial independence; and that rigid insistence upon unerring accuracy which is recognized as the chief characteristic of all Dodge Brothers' work."

This statement proclaims two simple concepts—first, that Dodge Brothers was an accomplished manufacturer in its own right as a large supplier, and second, Dodge Brothers' expertise and commitment to quality would be brought to bear on every car the company would now produce.

The very first ad for the car simply stated, "It Speaks for Itself." The tagline was followed by a list of the general specification and a picture of the car.

Later ads extolled the looks of the car or ease of operation, but the underlying theme stressed the specifications of the car and its advantages over the competition, like the all-steel body and enamel paint. The paint in particular was a selling point since it was baked on rather than brushed, as was the practice at other automakers. Dodge boasted "The result is a fast glossy finish of a peculiar elasticity which renders it practically impervious to wear or even ordinary damage."

Above: The original ad announcing that Dodge Brothers would build its first automobile is the picture of simplicity.

Right: As the division approached its 50th anniversary, this ad chronicled the evolution of Dodge cars from the very first model.

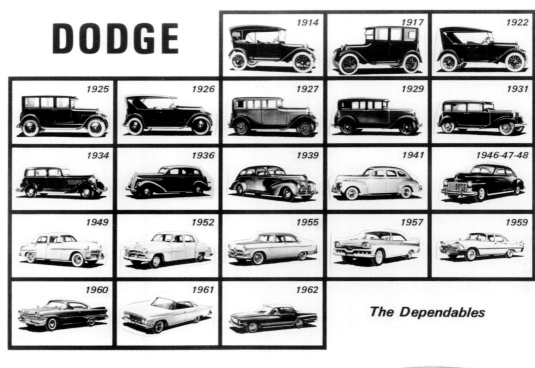

**1963 DART GT**

**1963 DODGE POLARA**

# Dodge Brothers
## TOURING CAR

Those who have driven the Touring Car longest are its most enthusiastic admirers.

They know from experience that with reasonable care it will serve the owner faithfully for many years.

Left: During the 1920s, a new advertising element was added: illustrations depicting the Dodge cars in everyday life.

Below, left: Early ads were the picture of simplicity, with an image of the car and a plainspoken message that stressed both the unchanging nature of the design and the low cost of operation.

Below, right: The investment bankers who owned Dodge were intent on moving the brand upmarket. Cars with 4-cylinder engines were dropped in favor of this family of sixes: the Senior, Victory, and Standard.

New Dodge Six Sedan $845

"I learned about women from Sarah Flint"

*a Dodge scout goes scouting*

THE SPIRITED NEW DODGE

*Beneath this Beauty*
DEPENDABLE VALUE

New Dodge Six and Eight are so impressive in beauty, comfort and power that upon this evidence alone they [a]rs of outstanding value. » » But they are truly *great* [be]cause of the even more important excellence beneath [su]rface—excellence that time alone can fully reveal. [T]he long life, the [econo]my, the dependa-

bility of the new Dodge cars are the result of long experience and the conviction that the most important thing about a motor car is that it be a *good* motor car. » » The New Six and Eight are already proving in the hands of owners that Dodge Brothers' most beautiful cars are also Dodge Brothers' greatest accomplishment in value.

Standard Dodge Eight Convertible Coupe, five wire wheels, $1095
© 1931 Dodge Brothers Corporation

New Dodge Six $815 to $845, New Dodge Eight $1095 to $1155, Standard Six $755 to $855, Standard Eight $995 to $1095. F. O. B. Factory. 5 wire wheels at no extra cost.

There were also ads that touted the integrity of the organization, including a 1917 statement characterizing the company as, "A stable institution with a stable product and a stable demand for the car. Three elements which make the business of Dodge Brothers a permanent, season-proof business."

Yet another ad stated, "The facts about the car and the men who build it need no embellishment." Dodge Brothers touted its 300,000 sales and characterized the owners as "300,000 builders of good will."

The popularity of the car had a lot to do with its dependability and durability, attributes that were underscored in the recurring catchphrase during this period that, "the gasoline consumption is unusually low. The tire mileage is unusually high."

During this period, Dodge also appealed heavily to the business car market with many ads showcasing the car's capabilities while stressing the low cost of operation.

# THE TIMES THEY ARE A-CHANGING

Long before Campbell Ewald dreamed up baseball, apple pie, and Chevrolet, Dodge was the embodiment of the American dream—affordable transportation for the upwardly mobile. It wasn't a luxury car for sure, but it also wasn't the cheapest on the market. It was solid, durable, and reflected the values of the bedrock middle class. In the early 1920s, this was reflected by Dodge's ads, which became more elaborate as time went on. They featured pastoral, Rockwellian imagery of family and friends engaging in everyday pursuits, particularly children involved in scouting, playing, or adopting a family dog.

Dodge Brothers had carefully staked out a sweet spot in the market, knew its buyers well, and embraced them. But that all began to change when Dillon, Read took over in 1925.

The new product binge and the move away from 4-cylinder to 6-cylinder cars, as well as the move upmarket with the Senior Six and Victory Six, foretold a distinct change in the advertising approach. Gone were the homey line drawings, replaced now with 4-color graphics showing young men and women in such non–middle class pursuits as polo, flying, and golf. When Walter Chrysler came onto the scene, Dodge vehicles were still being marketed to a more upscale audience since DeSoto was positioned between Dodge and entry-level Plymouth.

Recognizing that the traditional Dodge market could be slipping away, Chrysler moved quickly to allay fears that the Dodge name would disappear forever. A 1929 campaign announcing the Dodge Six heralded, "A great new model with a good old name."

The 1930s saw more economic turmoil as the result of the Great Depression. More importantly, though, it was time

Above: As the Great Depression wore on, marketing efforts reflected the tenor of the times with the message that Dodge was both dependable and affordable.

Left: Design became a major selling point in the 1930s, as shown by this ad touting the sleek shape of the exterior and interior appointments that "will thrill any woman." The ad also boasts that the car has a ride rivaling more expensive American and European cars.

Never Such Proof...Such Value

of great technical advancement and social change. The economics of the time gave new relevance to traditional Dodge selling points—the ads again stressed dependability and product advancements, like the line: "To Be Up To Date, Your Car Should Have Hydraulic Brakes."

This message of dependability dovetailed with Chrysler's decision to again reposition Dodge as a bridge between entry-level Plymouth and DeSoto, which now would be the steppingstone to Chrysler. This strategy promised to return Dodge to more familiar turf as a step-up car rather than a premium model.

In getting back to the basics, Dodge touted product features like its floating suspension, automatic clutch, and fuel-saving freewheeling to stress the ease of operation and low operating costs. This appealed to women and addressed the overall tenor of the Depression.

In 1942, with wartime fuel rationing an everyday reality, Dodge conducted fuel economy tests on 720 new vehicles in 600 cities. The results, shown in an ad touting "Take a Look at These All-American Scores," reported an average fuel economy of 21.6 miles per gallon, with state averages ranging from 17.6 in Rhode Island to 23.7 in Arkansas.

Above: The last civilian Dodge vehicles were promoted for their fuel economy at a time when wartime gas rationing was being implemented. The mileage returned would be respectable even today.

Below: The last major makeover of the Dodge lineup before World War II was introduced in 1940 with ads that demonstrated the practical aspects of the car, such as the ease of getting in and out and the improved engine power.

Alive with Innovations!

# 1940 DODGE with NEW FULL-FLOATING RIDE

# WHAT DODGE IS GOING TO DO

★

Again and again, from one end of the country to the other, the question is continuously asked — "What's Dodge going to do?"

The same question has been asked down the thirty years since the days of John and Horace Dodge at every turning point in the history of the motor car, —"What's Dodge going to do?"

Today's answer is — Dodge is starting production on the finest passenger car in its history. It is not an experimental car. It is as sound and certain a product as thirty years of leadership experience can make it.

If you know the immediate background of these new cars, you will recall that fully Certified Public Tests established for the last pre-war Dodge cars a public record in economy and performance that remains unchallenged to this day.

If you pause to think again, you will recall that Dodge All-Fluid Drive was an abrupt turning point in the technical development of all cars, giving an entirely new quality of automobile driving and performance.

The new Dodge will continue this brilli... The styling of the new car will be in sm... with the fluid smoothness of its perfor... have already shown that in economy... another record breaker.

## DODGE
### Division of Chrysler Corporation

New Thursday Night Program! The Music of Andre Kostelanetz with the most Popular Stars of the Musical World, Thursdays CBS.

Left: In returning from military production to building civilian cars, Dodge brought back the same body styles it sold some four years earlier. This ad stressed that the cars would be a proven commodity and not "an experimental car," possibly a veiled swipe at Preston Tucker.

## RIDE in the new Dodge!

## ..TWO DARING NEW MODELS THAT EVERYONE'S TALKING ABOUT !

*Bigger Three Ways*

LONGER on the inside . . . SHORTER outside!
WIDER on the inside . . . NARROWER outside!
HIGHER on the inside . . . LOWER outside!

The Exciting New Dodge MEADOWBROOK

Here's the car that dares to be different! It's the new Dodge—bigger three ways! Longer . . . wider . . . higher on the inside to give you extra head room and leg room. Yet on the outside it is actually shorter, narrower, lower to make all handling easier!

Windshield is larger . . . doors open wide for easier entry. Seats are many inches wider . . . "knee-level", too, for full leg support. You ride relaxed . . . comfortably "cradled" between the axles. In the new Dodge, your comfort comes first!

Powering both the new Dodge Coronet and new Dodge Meadowbrook is the famous Dodge "Get-Away" Engine . . . high compression engineered for extra power and greater gasoline economy.

Ride it, drive it! See how much more your money buys in the daring new Dodge!

The Beautiful New Dodge CORONET

"KNEE-LEVEL" SEATS give the natural distribution of body weight that makes the modern living room chair so comfortable.

DOORS OPEN WIDE—you step in or out without wrinkling or mussing clothes. Arm rest is on door . . . out of way.

"GET-AWAY" ENGINE—for flashing pickup, faster acceleration. High-compression engine gives greater gasoline economy.

*The Daring New*
## DODGE
gyrol Fluid Drive plus GYRO-MATIC
Frees You from Shifting
OPTIONAL ON CORONET MODELS

...ERYTHING YOU NEED TO KNOW

...about the new Dodge car is that it gives you all of ... combined advantages of Floating Power, All-Fluid ...ive, and Full Floating Ride.

...You get a cushioned, fluid quality of handling and ...formance which protects the life of the car indefinitely,

insures your safety and greatly improves riding and driving comfort.

The new Dodge speaks so well for itself, in style and performance, it seems silly to labor the subjects with more words of description.

Production is improving. If you have to wait a while for delivery, we sincerely thank you for your patience and promise you this very rich reward.

## NEW *Dodge*
### SMOOTHEST CAR AFLOAT

Left: It wasn't until early 1949 that the first all-new Dodge debuted. The new style featured front and rear fenders almost completely integrated with the body.

Above: The first postwar Dodge vehicles featured different grilles and other exterior trim items, but otherwise they were virtually the same as the 1942 models. Advertising reverted to color illustrations with family-oriented themes.

Above: The La Femme included a raincoat, hat, umbrella, handbag, cigarette case, and lighter, as well as a special paint scheme and matching interior colors.

Right: Little advertised, Dodge primarily promoted La Femme through brochures that featured pink as a primary color.

*La Femme*

now for the first time anywhere, a car glamorously, *Personally Yours*

Never a car more distinctively feminine than *La Femme* . . . first fine car created *exclusively* for women! In this superbly designed car, Dodge brings together luxurious, delicately-toned interiors and ultra-fashionable appointments . . . every sophisticated touch your heart could desire! Here is, truly, the ultimate in fine motoring.

*La Femme* by DODGE

BY APPOINTMENT TO HER MAJESTY . . . the *American Woman*

That test was cited again in postwar advertising under the banner, "What Is Dodge Going to Do?" as it returned to production of the cars that it had been building before the war's disruption. The company promised it "is starting production on the finest passenger car in its history. It is not an experimental car." Though odd, this disclaimer may have been a veiled swipe at Preston Tucker and his Tucker 48. The ad continued: "If you know the immediate background of these new cars, you will recall that fully Certified Public Tests established for the last prewar Dodge vehicles a public record of economy and performance that remains unchallenged to this day."

In these postwar years, the ads began to stress less the technical features and focused more on the car's role in the family, again accompanied by images of everyday people going about their daily business. By 1949, when the first all-new models began to appear since the war, the Daring New Dodge tagline appeared. And with the introduction of the Red Ram HEMI V-8 engine in 1953, Dodge returned to more traditional feature-oriented advertising, touting HEMI engine power or the vehicle's styling.

In the late 1940s and early 1950s, the Ram mascot appeared in the ads as a cartoon character. His run lasted until the mid-1950s, when design chief Virgil Exner—no big fan of the mascot— gave it the heave-ho with the 1956 model (though its use was retained on the truck models).

The next big change in advertising came in 1954 when actual photographs of the cars began to appear in place of line drawings and other artwork, although that practice would continue intermittently though the 1960s.

Above: The backs of the front seats of La Femme featured storage bins for the rain gear and handbag.

## "HER MAJESTY, LA FEMME!"

Throughout its history, Dodge had long pitched its products to women, again citing the dependability and ease of operation, especially with features ranging from standard electric starters up through the development of fully automatic transmissions.

In these endeavors, the company is probably best remembered for building the Dodge La Femme, a special edition of the Custom Royal Lancer in 1955 and 1956. Inspired by a pair of his-and-her Chrysler bubble-topped show cars developed in 1954 called the La Comtesse and Le Comte, La Femme featured a pink and pale gray color scheme, while Le Comte was painted a more masculine bronze and black.

For 1955, the La Femme was introduced. "By appointment to her majesty, the American woman" proclaimed the showroom brochures. The July 1955 issue of Popular Mechanics headlined an item, declaring, "Dodge La Femme is the first automobile with a gender—It's female!"

For $143, "her majesty" would get a car painted Heather Rose and Sapphire White, featuring upholstery and carpets in similar pink tones. The car came equipped with a rain hat, coat, and umbrella, as well as a pink leather handbag. The handbag stored a compact, lipstick case, coin purse, comb, cigarette lighter, and cigarette case. Both the raingear and the handbag could be stowed in special storage bins attached to the back of the front seats.

The La Femme returned in 1956 (this time with only the rain gear) and featured a Misty Orchid-over-Regal Orchid paint scheme. The interior dash matched the exterior paint scheme, and a new headliner reflected the materials used on the upholstery and carpet.

Below, left: Design chief Virgil Exner's "Forward Look" featured clean, modern shapes punctuated by large tailfins. It was first introduced to the public with the launch of the 1955 Dodge, but Exner's influence was much more dramatic on the 1956 models. Also of note was the fact that the Ram mascot had disappeared in favor of the new Forward Look emblem.

Below, right: The late 1950s were truly an era of excess. The large tailfins, two-tone paint schemes, and heavy reliance on chrome were simply ostentatious. However, a sharp recession and changing tastes soon spelled the end to the Swept-Wing look.

The neighbors will think you've hit the jackpot when you drive home in your new Dodge Dart. Dart is so smart and stylish it looks like it costs a pile of money. The fact is Dart is priced down with the lowest.* And Dart's Economy Slant "6" really stretches gas. So don't keep the neighbors in the dark. Give them the happy facts about Dart. Please?

## DART: So much fun for so little money!

**People are amazed** that the Dodge Dart is in the low-price field—it's so roomy and comfortable and luxurious. And Dart's one-piece all-welded Unibody construction is far stronger, protected against rust with seven rustproofing baths. Result? Dart stays tight and new and showroom bright years longer. For a sound investment, put your money on Dart.

*Dodge Dart is priced model for model with other low-price cars*

| DODGE DART | CAR F | CAR P | CAR C |
|---|---|---|---|
| SENECA | Fairlane | Savoy | Biscayne |
| PIONEER | Fairlane 500 | Belvedere | Bel Air |
| PHOENIX | Galaxie | Fury | Impala |

AMERICA'S 1st FINE ECONOMY CAR **DODGE DART**

DODGE DIVISION OF CHRYSLER CORPORATION BUILDS TWO GREAT CARS: DODGE DART • '60 DODGE

Above: Virgil Exner didn't care for the Ram mascot and replaced it with the Forward Look arrow theme.

Left: Even though the Dart had vestigial fins, this all-new model now rode on an intermediate chassis and the advertising returned to highlighting the value of owning a Dodge.

Below: The Forward Look emblems eventually gave way to this three-pointed emblem known as the Fratzog, which was used on Dodge products through the 1960s.

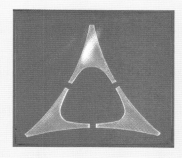

The La Femme was not widely advertised nor a big seller. Because it was part of the Custom Royal Lancer lineup, individual model sales are not broken out. Best estimates imagine that about 2,000 or so La Femmes were built. While the La Femme can be viewed as a product of its time, it spoke volumes about the role of women in not only influencing but also buying cars in postwar America. Dodge has long recognized the importance of women and their needs, from its earliest ads up through the development of the minivan.

As Dodge neared its 50th anniversary, a 1963 ad summed up nearly a half century of marketing by showing several Dodge models stretching back to the company's founding. The tagline was simple and effective. It read, "The Dependables." It was a message that resonates to this day.

# CHAPTER 5

# DODGE: DEFENDER OF DEMOCRACY

This Dodge 6x6 was the largest truck built for the United States Army.

War came slowly to America. It was more than two years after Germany invaded Poland on September 1, 1939, that the United States officially entered the war following the Japanese attack on Pearl Harbor.

World War II was responsible for no new Dodge cars on the road for nearly four years—the last model year of civilian car production, 1942, saw about 60,000 units produced. Still, Dodge, with its manufacturing capabilities, and its truck expertise in particular, played a pivotal role in the war's outcome.

Well before U.S. involvement in World War II, the company had begun production of military trucks for the government in the 4x4 VC model in 1940. But it wasn't the first Dodge to be used by the army.

The company had a long history of supplying vehicles and armaments to the military. Among the first to use Dodge vehicles was General John "Blackjack" Pershing, who obtained a fleet of 250 vehicles in his 1916 Mexican campaign against Pancho Villa. This expedition established Dodge's reputation for durability. One of his officers who swore by the capabilities of the Dodge product was George S. Patton, who led a daring raid using three Dodge vehicles to speed over a mile long road in a surprise attack. According to Charles Hyde in *The Dodge Brothers: The Men, The Motor Cars, The Legacy*, Patton is reported to have said, "We couldn't have done it with horses. The motor car is the modern war horse."

The WC's basic configuration was a 4x4 truck with an open back and cab. Canvas was used to cover the back and cockpit from the elements.

Pershing continued to use Dodge vehicles after the campaign, shipping them to France when the United States became involved in World War I in 1917. According to Dodge Brothers literature, some 12,795 vehicles were used in the war. Over 8,000 were touring cars, as well as 2,600 commercial vehicles, including screen-side and panel van models. They served primarily as ambulances and repair trucks, and all were highly regarded for their dependability and toughness.

But it wasn't the only contribution to the war effort for Dodge Brothers. The company was noted for its precision machining and was awarded a contract by the War Department to make recoil mechanisms for two 155mm cannons made by the French. These mechanisms, called hydropneumatic recuperators, were intricate mechanisms that were only made in France and in very limited numbers—just five per day.

John Dodge turned down an offer from the French manufacturers to send their craftsmen over to teach Dodge workers how to build the mechanisms. John reportedly refused the help, saying that he and Horace only needed the blueprints to do the work.

The command car underscores the versatility of the Dodge wartime truck lineup.

Dodge built the Lynch Road plant, and with a workforce of 1,800, was soon building 35 recoil mechanisms a day. In all, they built 1,601 for the Schneider howitzer and 881 for the Fillous general purpose gun. It was a remarkable feat, especially when the howitzer mechanism started from a rough forging weighing 3,875 pounds and resulted in a finished product that tipped the scales at just 870 pounds.

Flash forward 25 years, and again Dodge was tasked with building war material. And once again, Dodge's reputation for precision machining played a major role in winning the government work.

Dodge was tasked with building a factory to produce 18-cylinder Wright Cyclone radial engines for the new B-29 Superfortress bomber. The B29 was the first bomber with a pressurized cabin in the army air force's fleet, and the flying fortress could soar at over 35,000 feet. It had a range of more than 5,000 miles, which was critical in the bombing campaign against Japanese industry.

Under the leadership of Fred J. Lamborn, who at the time was vice president in charge of Dodge, a new assembly plant was built on Chicago's southwest side. It covered 30 city blocks with 6.3 million square feet of floor space in a 19-building complex. Although it just built aircraft engines—the airframes were produced elsewhere—Dodge-Chicago built all the parts of the engine in-house, absorbing ingots of aluminum and magnesium and churning out complete aircraft engines.

The plant manufactured a total of 18,413 engines by the end of the war, or about five engines each for the 3,628 Superfortresses that were built for wartime service.

Decommissioned after the war, the empty plant played a role in Preston Tucker's ill-fated bid to build the Tucker 48, or as it was more commonly known, the Torpedo. He had leased the sprawling facility from the government to build his dream car, but failed after producing only 51 units—48 of them actually built at Dodge-Chicago.

The plant was re-commissioned during the Korean War to again make aircraft engines—this time for jets—but it was Ford and not Dodge who had the contract. When the plant shut down in the late 1950s, it was revived as an industrial/commercial district, which included Chicago's first indoor shopping mall called Ford City. What's left of the original complex is also home to the candy maker Tootsie Roll.

## TEN MINUTE BREAK

Minutes of rest in the forward advance. Men from the States sprawled in the sunlit grass. Thoughts of home and gossip of battle. The big Dodge truck ready for action while the men await the signal for another push.

CHRYSLER CORPORATION

PLYMOUTH • DODGE • DE SOTO • CHRYSLER

JOIN THE ATTACK—BUY MORE WAR BONDS

Above: Using a sketch from a soldier, this Dodge war ad played on a recurring theme of the company's products earning the company's reputation for durability on the field of battle.

Right: The front of the Dodge-Chicago plant housed the administrative offices.

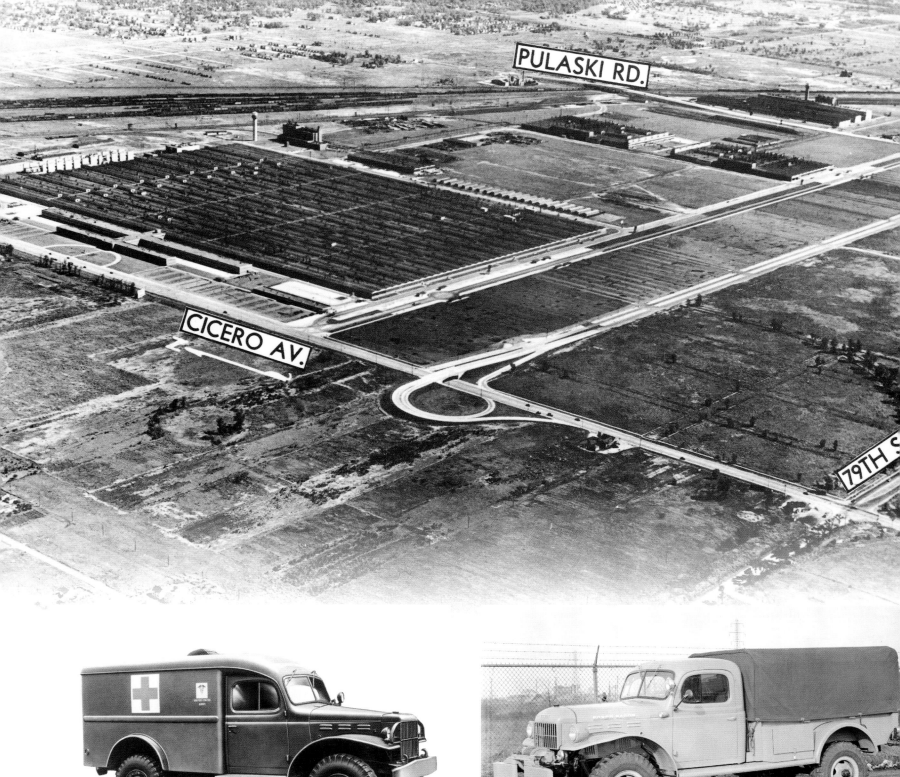

PULASKI RD.

CICERO AV.

79TH S.

Above: Another application of the WC54 4x4 truck was as an ambulance.

Above: A postwar version of the Power Wagon shows that it made the transition to civilian use with few modifications.

Top: This sprawling plant was built by Dodge on Chicago's southwest side to produce engines for the B-29 Superfortress. Preston Tucker used the facility after World War II to build his ill-fated car.

### Three Hundred Thousand Strong!

It's hard to get three hundred thousand Army trucks into any kind of picture. They take up as much room as several million soldiers...Of course they are now scattered all over the world behind the battle lines and on the fighting fronts. They range from the husky six-wheeled BIG SHOT down to the smaller weapons carriers and command reconnaissance cars. They include thirty thousand ambulances—official Army vehicles of medical rescue on practically every front. All of these Army trucks are direct descendents of the famous Dodge (job-rated) trucks of peacetime. Great has been the honor to Dodge of serving the Army in such a large and vital way. And great, also, is the responsibility!

**DODGE** DIVISION OF CHRYSLER CORPORATION
LET'S ALL BACK THE ATTACK — BUY MORE WAR BONDS
TUNE IN ON MAJOR BOWES EVERY THURSDAY, CBS, 9 P.M., E.W.T.

Above: The Power Wagon was developed in the closing days of World War II based on the 4x4 WC chassis.

Below: The radial engines go through the final stages of assembly at the Dodge-Chicago plant. More than 18,000 engines were built at the facility.

Above: During the war, Dodge produced many of the trucks used by the U.S. Army. This ad boasts of production that had passed the 300,000 mark.

Dodge's other military contracts during the war included making 8.3 million aluminum forgings for use in aircraft fuselages, and also manufacturing 2-speed gearboxes, gyro compasses, and even radar units. But the greatest contribution Dodge made to the war effort was its trucks.

Dodge had been building 4x4 trucks since 1934, and while the all-wheel drive configuration was not unique to the industry, the division was the first to actually put the lever that engaged 4-wheel drive in the cabin.

The VC line of trucks was developed in 1939, the first units rolled off the assembly line in 1940, and soon they were replaced by the upgraded WC. Among the configurations of this ½-¾ ton 4x4 and ½-1½ ton 4x2 trucks were command cars and weapons carriers, ambulances, and reconnaissance, utility, and radio vehicles.

The basic WC spec called for a 4x4 vehicle built on a 116-inch wheelbase (ambulances were longer at 123 inches) powered by an inline 6-cylinder engine. The engine was 230 cubic inches and produced anywhere from 78 to 99 horsepower. The WC was equipped with hydraulic brakes, a 4-speed manual transmission, and a 1-speed transfer case. The WC62-63 models, which featured a longer chassis, had dual rear axles and 6-wheel drive and could carry payloads of up to 3,300 pounds.

A November 1942 review in *Popular Science* reported that the WC trucks, when compared to the Jeep® brand, were "bigger, stronger, with high road clearance, a wide tread, splendid fordability of streams, and great tractive power through its 'high flotation' tires." The article also notes that these trucks were not just for behind-the-lines work: "it is for use on the fighting fronts as a tactical vehicle."

The Dodge WC truck series proved to be durable, dependable, and thanks to production that topped 250,000, seemingly ubiquitous in war zones around the world.

Above: Open Dodge WC51 4x4 trucks await shipment from the assembly plant to the war zone. The all-wheel drive capabilities of the WC made it ideal for tactical frontline use.

Above: Unlike the earlier open WC models, the Power Wagon had a closed cab similar to prewar pickup trucks, making it much more attractive to the postwar civilian market. Above is one of the rare few examples to be fitted with a canvas covering, which was not a factory option.

Left: Dodge's reputation for precision machining was instrumental in winning the contract to produce these 18-cylinder Wright Cyclone engine.

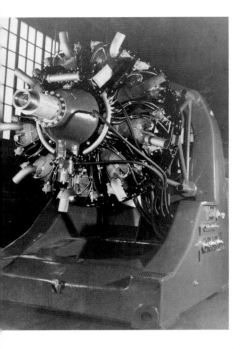

# ENTER THE POWER WAGON

While the 6x6 truck was used to help open the Burma Road to supply China, a later contract to build another truck for that country was responsible for the creation of an iconic Dodge that would see great success after the war—the Power Wagon.

In late 1944, Chiang Kai-shek asked the U.S. government for 15,000 vehicles to help resupply his National Chinese troops. The government awarded Dodge the contract to build the vehicles to the general's specification.

The vehicle had to be right-hand-drive and be powered by a large I-6-cylinder engine with a 5-speed manual transmission. Those specs matched one of the prototype trucks built by Dodge in 1939 using a conventional pickup cab, as opposed to the WC series trucks, which had in many cases featured an open or canvas covered cockpit.

Dodge built these trucks for China and then at the end of the war converted the design to left-hand drive. The first variant was the civilian version of the closed Carryall, which is similar to a modern SUV. It was called the Battle Wagon. The pickup version was then launched as the Farm Utility Vehicle in early 1946. Later on that year, it was renamed the Power Wagon, and the M-37—introduced in late 1950—was based on it. In addition to its rugged looks and 4-wheel drive, the Power Wagon offered power takeoff units on both front and rear axles, which allowed the user to run an optional front-mounted winch or auxiliary machinery in the field. The ads of the day called the Power Wagon "A Self-Propelled Power Plant." These civilian versions were equipped with a 94 horsepower I-6-cylinder engine, 4-speed transmission with 2-speed transfer case and heavy-duty off-road tires.

The Power Wagon is considered the first all-new postwar vehicle for the civilian market when it was introduced in 1946. It was a fixture in Dodge's lineup. There were two versions, the classic one from 1946 to 1968 and a more conventional body introduced in 1961, and it was redesigned in 1972. The last truck to use the Power Wagon name was released in 1980.

Like the veterans returning from war to resume civilian life, the Power Wagon helped with the transition of the truck lineup from military use to the consumer market. The postwar era for Dodge had begun.

Top: An 18-cylinder Wright Cyclone engine is mounted to a test stand at Dodge's Chicago factory.

Above: The Carryall version of the WC is the forerunner of the modern full-size sport utility vehicle.

Right: The all-purpose nature of the WC saw it used for a number of applications during the war (in this case as a weapons carrier).

# CHAPTER 6

# A TRUCK STORY

The introduction of the Power Wagon right after World War II speaks volumes about Dodge's expertise in trucks. Not only did the division's products have a proven track record in military use, but the assembly lines could be quickly geared to supply a civilian market hungry for vehicles. While it would take at least three years to tool up an all-new passenger car, Dodge was ready to deliver new trucks once hostilities ceased.

The trucks' roots extended all the way back to the company's founding in 1914. In those early days, there was little that differentiated cars from trucks. The basic engine and chassis were the same; the primary differences were in the body perched atop the frame. Just three years after the introduction of their first car, the Dodge Brothers introduced a delivery vehicle with screen sides in 1917 as a 1918 model. Within six months, a panel-side version of the same vehicle was

Looking like a half-car, half-truck hybrid, the 1934 Dodge KC pickup shared the car lineup's front clip, complete with Ram mascot.

these commercial vehicles for use by the army in World War I. Even after that war, the commercial business continued to grow to over 10 percent of annual production with the screen-side model accounting for more than half the business.

But, it was a small Indiana company flying under the radar that eventually provided the impetus for Dodge to become a major player in the truck market.

## BAND OF BROTHERS: DODGE AND GRAHAM

Three brothers—Joseph, Robert, and Ray Graham—had made a fortune in the glass business developing automatic bottle-making machines. When they sold their interests to Libbey-Owens Sheet Glass Co. (Toledo, Ohio), the trio from Evansville, Indiana, became interested in developing and selling tractors and trucks for agriculture. One of their first inventions was a new rear axle and frame that could convert a standard Ford Model T into a stake truck with a 1-ton payload.

This led to a lucrative business in converting Model T chassis into trucks, and in 1917 they named their concern Graham Brothers Truck Builder. In addition to modifying the rear axles and frames, the Grahams began to build cabs, stake beds, and panel bodies to fit on the altered chassis. These work trucks boasted payloads of up to 3 tons.

By 1919, Graham Brothers was building a 1½-ton truck of their own design called the Speed Truck in which they used Dodge Brothers engines and transmissions because of their durability.

The sales volume of these drivetrains through a small Indiana dealership eventually caught the attention of Dodge management in Detroit. Frederick Haynes, who had taken over as president in the wake of the Dodge brothers' deaths, struck a deal in 1921 with Graham Brothers to not only exclusively supply them with components, but also to open up the Dodge dealer network to them for national sales and service.

In one fell swoop, Dodge's truck offerings grew from simple commercial vehicles based on car chassis—which were branded Dodge—to a full range of trucks that could haul up to 2-ton payloads, which were sold under the Graham nameplate. By 1925, Dodge's commercial business had grown to nearly 60,000 units and trucks sales accounted for about a quarter of total production that year.

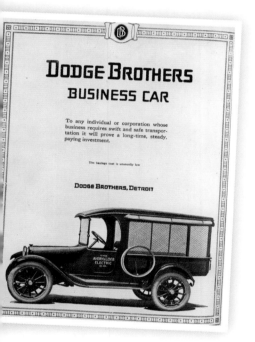

Above: Trucks have been very much a part of Dodge since the beginning, as this 1918 commercial vehicle ad demonstrates. The screen-side truck pictured here also came in a panel version.

Right: While the Graham Brothers acquisition helped to expand Dodge's truck lineup, light-duty commercial vehicles continued to be based off of car chassis, as was this 1932 half-ton panel truck.

Above: With front and rear power take-off units, the 1946 Dodge Power Wagon had a number of uses, including the ability to plow a field.

Top, left: This humpback version of the 1936 Dodge panel truck featured a raised roof for greater load-carrying capacity. Throughout the '30s, Dodge relied on Chrysler and Plymouth engines for its truck line, though they were upgraded for commercial use. Dodge also introduced the concept of "job-rated" trucks specified for particular tasks.

Bottom, left: The B-Series pickup, introduced in 1946, was equipped with 6-cylinder engines. The B-2, introduced in 1951, can be distinguished by its split-front windshield.

Above: The 1954 Dodge pickup was designated the C-Series and had a single-piece front windshield, while the back quarter windows were eliminated when the rear window was enlarged in 1955.

Below: The D-Series pickups replaced the C-Series in 1957. This '58 model, with the flush Sweptside cargo box, also sports carlike tailfins.

Above: One of the distinguishing characteristics of the B-Series was its "pilot house" cab that featured rear quarter windows. The extra glass gave the Dodge pickup great visibility out the rear.

Following Dodge Brothers sale to Dillon, Read & Co. in 1925, the new management executed an earlier plan to buy a controlling stake in Graham Brothers and eventually acquired the entire company. The Graham brothers became members of the Dodge board of directors, but after being paid more than $15 million, the three brothers left to start their own car company. Despite having management roles in Dodge, the trio soon figured out they would never be calling the shots. The Grahams purchased struggling Paige-Detroit Motor Car and renamed it Graham-Paige Motors.

Meanwhile, Dodge continued to sell trucks under the Graham nameplate until 1929 when it was discontinued after Chrysler took over.

That year was also the last year that Dodge relied on its in-house resources to build a pickup truck. Dodge offered three engines for the truck: a 45-horsepower 4-cylinder engine from Maxwell; and two Dodge I6 engines making either 63 or 78 horsepower. One of the technical innovations was the use of the standard hydraulic brakes when most pickups came only with mechanical binders.

The 1933 pickup line was redesigned and designated the HC (the C being a truck designation that would continue through the World War II WC). As part of the Chrysler corporate structure, Dodge trucks relied on engines from Plymouth and Chrysler, though with specific modifications designed to enhance durability. Two years later, the ½-ton pickup was joined by ¾- and 1-ton models.

Dodge redesigned the medium-duty trucks in 1936 with the MD. This version had a longer wheelbase, with the front axle moved forward to allow for a longer bed. Dodge also moved away from a traditional car-type frame to a heavier unit that used crossmembers in a ladder configuration.

Styling continued to evolve—essentially the look of Dodge pickups echoed the front clip of the passenger car lines. In addition to another redesign in 1939, Dodge also introduced the concept of a "Job Rated" pickup that allowed the buyer to design the proper specification to match the work for which the truck was intended.

By the 1960s, the fin fad was over for trucks as well. This '64-model Sweptline had a flush box design that would be used over a decade. The only changes to the D-Series were new grilles and a switch from dual to single headlamp units.

The trucks in the A-100 line were primarily built as cargo and passenger vans, but there was also a pickup among them. This '64 model shows why the vehicle is called "forward control": most of the cab is ahead of the front wheels.

The Dodge A-100 van series was quite flexible, offering cargo versions as well as people carriers like this Sportsman model. Note how far forward the steering column is from the front axle.

While the Power Wagon was an off-road 4x4 truck with a pickup bed, it was not part of Dodge's regular postwar pickup truck line. These 2-wheel-drive versions were called the B series, which debuted in 1948. This was also about the time the first all-new postwar Dodge cars were debuting.

The B-series trucks were quite popular for their so-called "Pilot House" design that featured a more upright seating position, and a larger glass area that included optional rear quarter windows to eliminate blind spots. Like the MD design, the front axle was again moved further forward, allowing most of the payload to be centered in the middle of the truck. The sides of the cargo box were made deeper to better secure the cargo. Inline 6-cylinder engines displacing 218 to 230 cubic inches powered the pickups.

In 1954, the pickups were redesigned, and the B series gave way to the C series. C series trucks were lower to the ground, featured trapezoidal grilles, and were distinguished by a single rather than two-piece windshield. These trucks were offered in 108-, 116-, and 126-inch wheelbases. 1954 was also the year that HEMI V-8 engine power was introduced, with both 241- and 331-cubic inch versions depending on the payload. While the HEMI engine was marketed as the Red Ram in the Dodge car lineup, in the trucks it was referred to as the Power Dome V-8 engine.

Dodge recognized that people were starting to use pickups for personal transportation in addition to work, so in 1972 it introduced a new facelift for its pickups, including this Adventurer model. These became known as lifestyle trucks.

A year after the C-series introduction, Dodge improved the truck to feature more carlike appointments, such as a fully automatic 2 -speed transmission in addition to the standard 3- and 4-speed overdrive manuals. The rear window now extended across the entire rear of the cab to improve visibility in the best Pilot House tradition, and the interior trim was upgraded.

Although the pickup was designed primarily for work, the C-series program was treated to nearly annual styling changes, which were industry practice on the car side of the business. In 1959, the truck was redesigned again and renamed the Power Giant. Among the styling modifications were the requisite tweaks to the grille, but the biggest change was the introduction of the new "Sweptline" pickup box option over the standard stepside configuration. The stepside cargo box had fenders over the back tires with the sides of the box inside the wheelwells. The new Sweptline box gave the truck a flush bodyside with wheelwells inside the box. In keeping with the fashion of the day, the Sweptline box also incorporated tailfins, adding to its more carlike appearance.

Left: Another truck innovation was the introduction of the Club Cab in 1973, which offered additional space behind the front seats. The personal-use truck market was about to explode.

Below: A two-tier approach to fuel economy and emission regulations that was more lenient towards trucks allowed the 1978 Dodge Lil' Red Express to be one of the quickest vehicles on the market. The name was a variation on the name Little Red Wagon, a '60s-era wheel-standing A-100 pickup.

Right: Looking to straddle the gap between traditional full-size pickups offered by Ford and Chevy and small compact pickups that were the mainstay of Japanese makes, Dodge introduced the mid-size Dakota pickup in 1987.

Right: While the Dakota did well in carving out a unique niche with its mid-size market position, Dodge decided it needed to make a dramatic statement in the full-size truck market. The Ram VTS concept of 1996 was a thinly disguised version of the all-new pickup.

Below: The Dakota proved to be a flexible platform, offering a number of variants. This convertible model was launched in 1989.

Technical advancements included power brakes, power steering, and pushbutton automatic transmission. Dodge also introduced a model numbering system of D100–900 to designate the vehicle's configuration and load-carrying capability.

The fin craze lasted but two years. By 1959, the Sweptside pickups sported smooth cargo boxes similar to those used on most pickups today. The other notable feature was that the lower door skins now concealed the truck's running boards. The 1960 model year saw another grille redesign, as the pedals were changed and suspended beneath the dash, replacing the floor-hinged setup.

The next generation of Dodge pickups was introduced in 1961 and now featured longer wheelbases across the board in 114-, 122-, and 133-inch variants. The frames were beefed up, and the Sweptline boxes redesigned to be 4 inches wider. Two Slant Six engines were offered: a 170-cubic-inch engine making 101 horsepower, and 225-cubic-inch unit with 140 horsepower. A 318-cubic-inch V-8 engine with 200 horsepower was optional.

By this time, the annual model change mania in the industry has cooled, especially in the truck segment. Still, Dodge announced that new features, like the use of alternators that recharged batteries at idle, would be added as they were developed rather than waiting until annual model changeover, a practice that John and Horace Dodge could appreciate.

The pickups received a grille change in 1962 and added a 4-door crew cab model to the lineup. Dodge saw its best truck sales performance since 1956 with over 108,000 sold. The next big styling change came in 1965 when the front end went to single headlamps instead of the dual units.

Dodge began to expand its truck offerings when it developed the A-100 and A-108 van family, a compact box on wheels that featured forward-control seating, where the dash and steering wheel were positioned ahead of the front wheels. Introduced in 1964, these vehicles mounted the engines between and below the front seats. Riding on a 90- or 108-inch wheelbase, the A-series could be powered by either a Slant Six or V-8 engine, and it was offered in pickup, panel,

Above: In taking the bold look of its trucks to the heavy-duty segment, Dodge introduced the Big Red Truck concept in 1998 to pave the way for its new range of work trucks.

Inset: The Dodge Ram debuted in 1994 with a stepped fender design that mimicked the look of semi-truck rigs. It helped move the division's market share into the double digits in full-size truck sales.

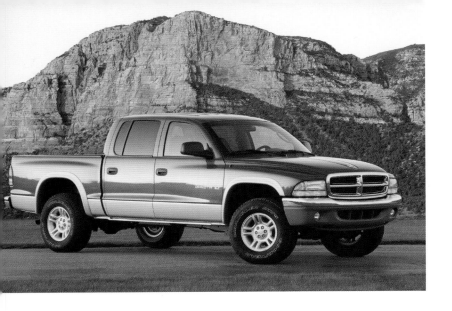

Above: Dodge continued to refine the Dakota, as this 2004 model shows. More carlike amenities and four conventional doors made this pickup a cargo and family hauler.

Below: So successful was the Ram that the bold looks of the full-size pickup were adapted for the Dakota, with positive results.

passenger, and camper van configurations. The popularity of this new model led to the demise of all pickup-based Town and Panel Wagon models in 1966. The A-100 and A-108 were built until 1971 when they were replaced by the larger B-van, which was produced from 1971 until 1998.

The next generation of Dodge pickups debuted in 1972 and was considered a "Lifestyle" vehicle because of the increasing personal use outside the work environment. While the trucks still maintained their reputations for durability, they were more often than not seen towing a boat or a camper as they were on a job site. The D-series pickups sported clean, simple lines, but also could be ordered in a two-tone paint scheme to give them more character. Three wheelbases were offered: 115-, 131-, and 133 inches, and engines included the Slant Six, and three V-8 engines with displacements ranging from 318 to 400 cubic inches.

While Dodge had been building crew cabs for a decade, in 1973 it introduced the Club Cab, a traditional 2-door pickup with a longer cabin that had additional storage and optional jump seats that provided greater utility; this was an industry first.

In keeping with this new emphasis on lifestyle trucks, Dodge developed a performance pickup that recalled the Lil' Red Truck wheelstanding A-100 of the 1960s. Introduced in 1978, the Lil' Red Truck was part of a larger marketing exercise that promoted adult toys (done up in black, the same truck was known as the Warlock). This pickup featured a stepside box and rode on the short 115-inch wheelbase. It also had a 360-cubic-inch V-8 engine beneath the hood with a 4-barrel carburetor that produced 225 horsepower. Because the rollout in emission standards had yet to affect light trucks, the Lil' Red Truck didn't require a catalytic converter. According to a test in *Car and Driver*, it was the quickest American-made production vehicle at the time, reaching 100 miles per hour in 19.9 seconds.

## DAKOTA SPLITS THE DIFFERENCE

Trucks have traditionally longer product cycles than cars, and the Dodge pickup was no exception, undergoing its next major change in 1981. Although the basic platform remained the same, the trucks received all-new sheetmetal, significantly upgraded cabins, and the designation Ram, resurrecting the mascot that had gone missing since the 1950s.

Although the trucks retained their durability and offered comparable drivetrains, performance, and load-bearing capabilities as Ford and Chevrolet models, Dodge pickups were never a major factor in the market. In the Dakota, though, Dodge sought to take a different tack by building a true mid-size truck that would offer far more capability than the compact trucks offered by both domestic and import makes.

In 1986, the Dakota was launched as a 1987 model in two wheelbases—112- and 124-inch—and in regular and extended cab, as well as short- and long-bed configurations. The base engine was a 2.2-liter 4-cylinder engine making 96 horsepower with an optional 3.9-liter V-6 engine featuring 125 horses. With nothing quite like it on the market, the Dakota was a hit, selling nearly 105,000 units.

Above: The 2010 Dodge Dakota Laramie showed not only that pickups had become personal transporters, but also that buyers expected the same level of accessories, features, and styling that they could get in luxury cars.

Inset: A postwar version of the Power Wagon shows that it made the transition to civilian use with few modifications.

This success, however, undercut the full-size Ram. Dodge hoped to reduce the complexity in Ram assembly by dropping the Club Cab. Dakota evidently took up the slack, and this new mid-size truck actually outsold all of Dodge's full size trucks combined. In its 25-year run before the model was discontinued in 2011, the Dakota spawned some interesting variants, including a convertible.

The decline in Dodge full-size pickups came at a time when the most popular selling vehicle on the market was the Ford F-150. Looking to break out of its single-digit share of this lucrative segment, Dodge staked out a bold strategy of designing its next truck with a polarizing look, rather than sticking to a conventional approach to design.

Borrowing a stepped fender look that recalled both rugged over-the-road semi tractors and Dodge's own postwar B-series pickup, the new Ram, codenamed T-300, was that bold statement. In marketing clinics it either scored extremely high or extremely low—there was nothing lukewarm about the reception. The people who loved the design, however, far outnumbered those who didn't, resulting in a net gain in sales.

The Ram was introduced as a '94 model with a 118.7-inch wheelbase and a standard cab. Engines ranged from a 3.9-liter V-6 engine to a 5.9-liter V-8 engine. Sales more than doubled to 240,000 in the first year. So successful was the look of the new Ram, that this retro approach to styling was adapted to the Dakota's second generation in 1997.

The Ram pickup proved to be so successful that in 2009 it would be spun off as its own operation that included not just pickups, but all of Chrysler's commercial vehicles. In a way, the Dodge truck experience has come full circle, from the integration of the Graham Brothers operation to giving birth to a new division called Ram.

The Power Wagon, thanks to its 4x4 drive, made an ideal towing platform.

# CHAPTER 7

COMPLETE DEPENDABILITY

The new Dodge is the first car in automobile
history to give you all of the combined advantages of Floating
Power, All-Fluid Drive and Full Floating Ride. A rich reward
for your waiting, the new Dodge has been well
named "The Smoothest Car Afloat."

# PEACE, PROSPERITY, AND POWER

With the first all-new postwar Dodge still a year away, the advertising in 1948 returned to the homey, illustrated style of the early 1930s, stressing dependability but not much else in terms of technical innovation.

The postwar era for Dodge, like all automakers who had stopped producing cars in order to make armaments for the war effort, began slowly.

Although design proposals for new models existed—including renderings for new grilles, more glass area, and so-called *envelope bodies* that integrated the fenders with the body structure—dramatic changes such as these were not implemented in favor of less costly changes to trim items that could be used on the existing 1942 models as a way to differentiate them from the prewar cars.

There were two reasons for this more conservative approach. The first was that the tooling was relatively new from the 1941 facelift. The second reason was more important for the future of Dodge—the manufacturing division could resume production more quickly if there were fewer changes to the cars themselves.

DODGE

The Wayfarer Three-Passenger Roadster

Above: When Dodge debuted the first all-new postwar vehicles in 1949, the lineup included a new short-wheelbase model called the Wayfarer, which was offered in coupe, sedan, and roadster body styles.

Below: While Chrysler took a chance with the 1934 Airflow, design at Dodge was more evolutionary and historically had followed rather than led. That would change when Virgil Exner took over design activities. Here, clay modelers sculpt a wagon version of the Forward Look cars.

That's not to say the 1946 models were identical to the '42s. The new models had different grille texture, the parking lamps were larger and square, and in Dodge tradition, there were more improvements under the skin than to the skin itself. Chief among these were moving the starter from a floor-mounted pushbutton to the dash, improvements to the transmission, and the use of better fuel and oil filters.

The demand for cars was high after a nearly four-year hiatus, coupled with the fact that those who had worked on wartime production lines and returning veterans had money in their pockets ready to spend.

Between 1946 and 1948, Dodge built 708,560 cars while busy working on an all-new replacement for the 1949 model year, even though some of the last cars built in late 1948 were called "first-series" '49 models until the all-new Dodge was launched in April 1949. The new look of the car was tall and slab-sided with less pronounced fenders. The transition from prewar cars that had standalone fenders and running boards was complete—the new design (although more square than the cars to follow and still employing bolt-on rear fenders) was the first major step toward the envelope body that integrated fenders, bodysides, and decklids.

While previous Dodge vehicles featured one of two wheelbases (either a 119.5-inch for a standard car or a 137.5-inch 7-passenger model), the new "second series" Dodge cars had longer standard wheelbases of 123.5 inches, an 8-passenger chassis riding on the 137.5-inch wheelbase, and a new 115-inch short wheelbase model in coupe, 2-door sedan, and roadster, called the Wayfarer. The 1949 models also introduced some other new model names: Meadowbrook, for the base 4-door sedan, and Coronet, for the higher trim levels. Also new and a first for Dodge was a woody wagon and a Coronet Diplomat hardtop coupe.

Beneath the hood, Dodge continued using the 230-cubic-inch I6, which made 103 horsepower. Behind the engine, however, buyers could opt for a standard 3-speed manual with a column-mounted shift or Fluid Drive transmission, which used a fluid coupling that eliminated clutch use in starts as well as up- and downshifts. This gearbox also had two ranges: low, which incorporated 1st and 2nd gear; and high, which had 3rd and 4th gears. The clutch was only used to shift between the ranges or when engaging reverse.

While production peaked in 1950 at 373,107 vehicles, the immediate postwar transition was not without its difficulties. Even though there was tremendous pent-up demand, the distribution of raw materials was still tightly controlled by the government, along with limits on civilian vehicle production.

Minor changes to styling were the norm until the 1953 model year, which marked not only a new car, but also a new approach to styling thanks to the influences of Virgil Exner, Chrysler's new design chief. A former associate of famed industrial designer Raymond Loewy, Exner joined Chrysler from Studebaker.

From a styling perspective, the 1953 model is significant for its total integration of the rear fenders for a smooth nose-to-tail body side, and the switch from a two-piece to a one-piece windshield. A short 114-inch-wheelbase model shared with Plymouth was the basis of the new entry-level Meadowbrook Suburban line. Also, the short-wheelbase platform was used for Coronet Eight models, which were equipped with the first V-8 engines in Dodge history.

Above, left: The 1953 model year saw the introduction of a new design for the Coronet that fully integrated the front and rear fenders into the body. It was also the first year for the Red Ram HEMI V-8 engine.

Above: Before the Forward Look was introduced in 1956, Dodge stressed the dependability and ruggedness of their cars. This 1952 ad prominently features the Ram mascot, which would soon disappear at Exner's insistence.

## THAT THING GOT A HEMI®? (PART 2)

The introduction of the Red Ram V-8 engine marked the beginning of a new era for Dodge. Not only did the brand continue its reputation as a builder of dependable cars, but it also became even more renowned for high performance.

The Red Ram V-8 engine was developed from the 331-cubic-inch Chrysler V-8 engine, which was introduced in 1951 and known as the HEMI engine for the shape of its combustion chambers—the hemispherical design did a better job of mixing fuel and air, which resulted in a more complete burn and better flow through the engine, resulting in higher performance and better fuel economy. Displacing 241 cubic inches, the Red Ram V-8 engine was rated at 140 horsepower, a significant boost over the 104-horsepower I6 in base models.

The engine's performance and fuel economy provided a promotional shot in the arm for Dodge. Using the Red Ram, a Dodge hit 23.4 miles per gallon in the Mobilgas Fuel Economy run—a number that topped the fuel economy of the 6-cylinder models from 1941.

Dodge started to participate in speed runs and racing with stock vehicles, the company's first real foray into motorsports. One of the racing successes for Dodge in the mid-1950s was taking the top four spots in its class at the 1954 Panamericana Road Race in Mexico.

Dodge and Dodge owners rejoiced; the new vehicles were an unprecedented hit.

The company boosted production to 342,047, although the number dropped by half the next year. In 1954, Dodge supplied its first pace car to the Indy 500. The pace car was named the Royal 500, and about 700 replicas were produced for the public.

Top: This second version of the Firearrow features a full top, wing windows, and roll-up side glass as part of a plan to put the vehicle into limited production. The idea was scrapped and the plans for the car sold to Eugene Casaroll, who built it as the Chrysler-powered Dual-Ghia.

Middle: Not all show cars came from Italy—Dodge commissioned the Granada concept from the Detroit firm Creative Industries.

Bottom: Two-tone paint schemes became a major trend throughout the 1950s. The roof of this 1954 Dodge Royal coupe contrasted with the lighter pastel color of the body.

This limited edition model cost $2,632 and included a 10-horsepower boost in output, a rear Continental kit for the spare tire, and Kelsey-Hayes wire wheels.

The performance of the Red Ram V-8 engine combined with the styling skills of Virgil Exner transformed Dodge during the 1950s. While Chrysler had dabbled in concept cars before World War II, those futuristic models were usually branded Chryslers. Exner commissioned a series of futuristic show cars for all the brands, many of which were built by Ghia, an Italian styling house. The first Dodge to appear was the Firearrow Roadster in 1953, followed by the Firearrow Sports Coupe a year later. The coupe rode on the longer 119-inch wheelbase, and this futuristic 2-door was equipped with a 150-horsepower Red Ram V-8 engine mated to a PowerFlite torque converter automatic transmission.

By mid-decade, Exner was finally having a profound impact on production car styling. The 1955 models were the first of these "Forward Look" cars, which addressed the criticism that Dodge vehicles seemed dumpy in comparison to the competition.

The clean look of the new cars, which had all models sharing a 120-inch wheelbase, was a dramatic change. The bodies were lower and wider with an aggressive shark-like nose that made the car appear that it was moving even when standing still. The lower body was offset by a larger glass area featuring thin pillars and a sleeker rake to the rear window.

Beneath the hood, the 6-cylinder engine now packed 123 horsepower, while the V-8 engine was upped to 270 cubic inches and came in three states of tune: 175, 183, and 193 horsepower. The model lines were trimmed to just Coronet, Royal, and Custom Royal models, and the Meadowbrook was eliminated. Dodge even regained some of the sales lost in 1954 with the new design, building 309,211 cars in 1955, maintaining that level of output until the recession of 1958.

Bottom: The big styling breakthrough for Dodge was the 1956 Forward Look, as shown in this Custom model. Large fins, thin pillars, and a sharklike nose gave the car a sleek and aggressive appearance.

Inset: The advertising for the new 1956 Forward Look Lancer was as bold as the design itself.

Man, it's Dynamite! '56 DODGE

# TALL TAILFINS, LONG LIGHTS, AND A WHOLE LOT OF CHROME

Above: The 1950s are also fondly recalled for such interesting features as the swivel seat and Highway Hi-Fi, a built-in record player.

Below: The Dodge Royal family in 1958 was all about fins, chrome, and road-hugging weight. These behemoths were launched as the economy slid into a severe recession, which not only cost Dodge sales, but also sealed the fate of DeSoto and Ford's new Edsel.

**American cars from this period are known principally for one thing—the tailfin—and Dodge was no exception to this rule.**

The other paradigm shift—especially given Dodge's long history of incremental changes to styling amidst constant product improvements—was the embrace of the annual styling change. The 1956 models built on the Forward Look design from a year earlier had taller fins and a more rakish roofline. Beneath the hood, the top-spec V-8 engine now displaced 315 cubic inches and made 218 horsepower. And pushbuttons instead of a column shift appeared for the 2-speed TorqueFlite automatic transmission.

In 1957, the cars changed again. This time, though, they displayed a complete redesign that featured a new torsion bar suspension and a longer 122-inch wheelbase. The new design was stunning; instead of two headlamps, four headlamps now framed the face of the vehicle above a wide, massive chrome front bumper that gave way to sleek lines down the body and massive tailfins at the rear. The rear of the car featured twin-stacked taillamps that looked like jet afterburners. The most attractive models were the 2-door hardtop coupes that had thin pillars and incredibly fast rakes to the rear windows.

The basic body shell remained the same through the 1959 model year with annual changes to the front grille. Engines continued to be upgraded through this period, culminating in the top-spec 383-cubic-inch V-8 engine in 1959 that produced 345 horsepower.

# CHAOS AND RENEWAL

The late 1950s was a tumultuous time in the industry. The economy, wracked by recession in 1958, saw industry sales plunge across the board. Dodge production in 1958–59 was less than half of what was produced in 1956–57, but there were also some significant, high-visibility failures, including the launch and fairly quick demise of the Edsel.

The Edsel was designed to bridge the gap between Mercury and Lincoln, but failed due to the controversial styling, bad economy, and an ill-defined market niche.

The same could be said, however, for Chrysler's DeSoto lineup. Positioned between Dodge and Chrysler, DeSoto became less relevant as Dodge benefited from improvements in styling and mechanical specifications. Dodge also had a strong dealer body, a longer history, and an ability to stretch its product range to cover the sliver of the market served by DeSoto. As a result, DeSoto was discontinued in 1961.

The poor economy in the late 1950s also saw a social backlash at what was perceived as conspicuous consumption embodied in these chromed and finned behemoths. Small imported cars from Europe were beginning to have an impact on the market, and Detroit decided that it needed to create a range of compact cars to counter this criticism and to take on the new competition from abroad.

The 1960 model year saw the debut of the Dart, which at the time was a large family car instead of the compact vehicle on the roads today. The difference was that these sedans and coupes had 118-inch wheelbases, which were 4 inches shorter than the standard 122-inch wheelbases of 1959. The larger platform was reserved for the Dart station wagons and two new models, the Matador and Polara.

Dodge's first true compact car, the Lancer, was introduced in 1961. It had a 106.5-inch wheelbase and came in two models (the 170 and 770) with a choice of two 6-cylinder engines—either a 170-cubic-inch unit making 101 horsepower, or a 225-cubic-inch I6 making 145 horsepower. These engines were called Slant Sixes since the cylinder bank was canted thirty degrees off vertical, which allowed for lower hood lines.

The Lancer was a handsome coupe and sedan. It featured a clean, uncluttered shape except for the large character lines that defined the front and rear fenders. These design cues influenced larger Dodge models in 1962; both the Dart and Polara were downsized with the Lancer's look onto a 116-inch wheelbase, while the Custom 880 (which was meant to be

the 1962 DeSoto) was introduced as the full-size entry on the previous year's 122-inch wheelbase.

As the 1960s progressed, the flamboyant styling of the 1950s faded. While both '60 and '61 Dodge cars still had tailfins, they were much more restrained, and by 1962 they entirely disappeared.

While the 1950s are known for their flash, a more lasting legacy of this era was the introduction of the Red Ram V-8 engine. The HEMI engine would come to define the very essence of Dodge performance throughout the 1960s, and the cars powered by this engine helped burnish the division's reputation for building fast cars that were poised to become cultural icons in their own right. The Dodge Rebellion was about to begin.

Above: The Dodge Main plant cranks out cars, having quickly transitioned from making parts for the war effort.

Below: The 1960 Dodge Dart put a fitting finish on the excesses of the '50s. Slightly smaller (but not by much), the Dart had vestigial tailfins. Within two years, the fins would be gone forever.

# CHAPTER 8

# DODGE DREAMIN'

If there were a design philosophy at Dodge Brothers when the first car rolled off the assembly line in 1914, it probably would have been "form follows function."

Basic in appearance and offered in only one color—black—the first Dodge automobile appealed to the public for its utility as a dependable transportation device. And in an era when the days of getting around with a horse were not far behind, a simple automobile like the Dodge was exotic in its own right.

For nearly 40 years, styling was a secondary consideration, especially after the 1934 Airflow underperformed for Chrysler, Imperial, and DeSoto. In contrast, design had moved into the forefront at General Motors under Harley Earl, who created the industry's first styling department in 1927. He is also credited with creating the first concept or dream car, the 1938 Buick Y-Job, a sleek roadster with hideaway headlamps. While Chrysler soon followed with its own show cars (the 1940 Newport Phaeton and the 1941 Thunderbolt), there were no similar Dodge dream cars to speak of.

The 1954 Dodge Firearrow Roadster was the first concept car in Dodge history and was used to showcase the introduction of the Red Ram HEMI V-8 engine.

# BACK TO THE FUTURE

That would all change with the arrival of Virgil Exner as head of design. Enamored with the styling and bespoke bodywork from Italian carrozzeria (Ghia in particular), Exner got the ball rolling with the 1951 Chrysler K-310. This one-off show car was designed to showcase the new 331-cubic-inch HEMI V-8 engine, the 310 denoting its horsepower.

Soon, there were show cars for all Chrysler divisions including Dodge. The first was the 1953 Dodge Firearrow, a sleek 2-seat roadster designed to showcase the recently introduced Red Ram HEMI V-8 engine. It was followed in quick succession by the Firearrow II and III, which included both a roadster (II) and a coupe (III) with similar bespoke bodywork on a standard 119-inch Dodge chassis with the 150 horsepower 241-cubic-inch HEMI engine beneath the hood.

The Firearrow IV was also exhibited in 1954. It was a 4-seat convertible with bodywork similar to the previous Firearrows. It had a checkered-flag motif on the seats, as well as a framed windscreen, roll-up windows, and a working top. The car seemed destined for production.

It was followed a year later with the Firebomb, which shared the same body. The Firebomb was painted black instead of red, and had some trim differences. It too appeared ready for a limited run, but it wasn't to be.

Instead, the design was sold to Detroit businessman Eugene Casaroll, who formed Dual Motors Company. Casaroll built the car at Ghia using Chrysler power, and a total of 104 Dual-Ghias were built between 1956 and 1959.

Not all the concepts came from Italy. Dodge showed off the Granada, a 1954 show car with an all-fiberglass body and was built by Detroit's Creative Industries. The Granada was likely a response to Chevrolet's Corvette and Kaiser's Darrin convertible, both of which were built using the new composite material.

Above: The cockpit of the Deora was accessed through a liftgate adapted from a Ford station wagon. The lower half rested on a pivot that swung to the side.

Right: The 1967 Dodge Deora didn't come from the design department but rather was the work of the Alexander brothers, a Detroit-based duo who built custom cars. The car won the prestigious Ridler Award at Autorama.

The 1961 Flitewing epitomizes mid-century space-age styling. Though not as ostentatious as some of the finned cars of the '50s, it still made extensive use of chrome ornamentation.

Inset: Perhaps the most distinctive feature of the Flitewing was its use of window and roof panel gullwings to ease entry and exit.

Top: The Deora's clean shape is every bit as contemporary today as it was when it debuted in 1967. The Mattel Hot Wheels Deora model is one of the most popular of all time.

Right: The open-top 1992 Viper roadster with its exposed side pipes was meant to recall the Shelby Cobra.

Below: The Dodge Charger III was a 1968 styling exercise that tested the waters for a possible Corvette rival. The front-engine, rear-drive 2-seater had a pop-up canopy that provided access to the cockpit.

After the Firearrow and Firebomb concepts, Dodge didn't display another concept until 1961 with the futuristic Flitewing. This experimental car, said to have cost $125,000 to build, featured swing-up gullwing side glass over conventional doors. The interior had pushbutton controls in the doors for the lights, turn indicators, windshield wipers, power windows, and power antenna. The speedometer featured a series of 13 windows in 10-mile-per-hour increments that lit up as velocity increased. Ghia built the body of the car, and the engine was a 383-cubic-inch V-8 engine making 330 horsepower.

After this flight of fancy, the concepts became a bit more rooted in reality. In 1964, the first concept for the Dodge Charger debuted. At the time, it was more of a roadster version of a Polara Coupe, and as a show car featured a cut-down windshield, no top, and a large, Targa-style bar. The Charger II concept, shown in 1965, was actually a version of the '66 production car that sported a longer tail and more aggressive front end that had exposed rather than hideaway headlamps.

Perhaps the most iconic concept car of this era was actually designed by some hot rodders who were given a pickup version of the new A-100 van series. Called the Deora (for Golden Dodge), this space-age beauty was created by Larry and Mike Alexander, known as the "A Brothers." Mike and Larry owned a custom car shop in Detroit, and it was there where the Deora took shape. Low and sleek, it didn't have conventional doors; instead, the windshield lifted up and the nose of the car swung sideways to allow access to the cabin. The Deora won the coveted Ridler Award at Detoit's 1967 Autorama, and it would become one of the most popular Hot Wheels models ever, with millions sold.

Dodge was back in 1968 with another futuristic concept, the Charger III. The Charger III was primarily an aerodynamic study, as Dodge had no plans to launch this 2-seat Corvette rival. The front-engine rear-drive study used a canopy rather than doors for access to the cockpit. Standing only 42 inches tall, the Charger III also had a steering wheel and instrument panel that swung upwards, making it easier to get in and out of the driver's seat. At the rear of the car, the body panels were actually air brakes that flipped up and out to help the car slow down.

Above: Based on the front-drive Omni O24 platform, the Stealth paved the way for the Daytona coupe and other front-drive performance cars from the division. One of its innovations was an early use of flush-mounted glass.

Below: Although the name was used on a 4-door sedan, the Intrepid concept featured a mid-mounted engine. Its shape influenced the Mitsubishi-built Stealth that debuted in 1991.

## REKINDLING THE DREAM

Through the rest of the 1960s and into the early 1970s, the show car circuit saw modified production cars, usually Targa-top or convertibles, like the Charger R/T and Challenger Yellowjacket, the latter of which was reworked and shown as the Diamante concept. Another one-off was the Daroo, a modified Dart by the self-proclaimed King of the Kustomizers, George Barris.

The nightmare that was the 1970s economy and energy shocks left little time and energy for dream cars. The main priority was survival. Once Chrysler regained its footing in the 1980s, it could again focus on the future.

The first show car of this era was the 1982 Stealth, an evolution of the Omni/Horizon-based O24/TC3 coupe. It had sharp angled lines reminiscent of the Lancia Stratos. Unlike that legendary mid-engine Italian exotic, the Stealth retained its front-engine, front-drive layout, and was powered by a 2.2-liter turbocharged I4 engine. One of the chief attributes of the design was its aerodynamic use of flush glass. Carroll Shelby also designed a hotrod version of the Dodge Rampage pickup based on the O24 platform and called it the Streetfighter. In addition to a tonneau cover over the cargo bed, the vehicle had a new nose with pop-up headlamps.

After Tom Gale took over the design staff in 1985, the approach to concept cars changed. The use of these dream cars was institutionalized—some show cars would be part of the new product development process, others would be used to test consumer reaction to new product niches, while some would be used to communicate a future direction in technology or design philosophy. But the one thing that Gale insisted upon was that the concepts would be rooted in reality—more often than not they were running prototypes.

Inset: The 1990 Dodge LRT, which stood for Little Red Truck, was a precursor to the radical styling approach later used on full-size Ram trucks in 1994.

Bottom: Based on Dodge Neon mechanicals, the Aviat concept was developed to test aerodynamic efficiency. Pylon-mounted and skirted rear wheels contribute to the car's slippery shape.

The first of these new Dodge concepts shown to the public was the Intrepid in 1988. While this 2-door mid-engine coupe bore the name of what would become the Dodge sedan flagship in the 1990s, the design itself was a precursor of the upcoming Dodge version of the Mitsubishi 3000GT, which would be called Stealth. Although it did point to a new product in the pipeline, the mid-engine 2-seat Stealth differed greatly from the front-engine 2+2 that eventually made production.

Left: When Dodge wanted to introduce a sporty, rear-drive coupe in its lineup, the Venom concept debuted in 1994 to a positive reception. Unfortunately, however, Dodge did not have access to a low-cost rear-drive platform to be able to put it into limited production.

Below: The interior of the Dodge Copperhead features a gated shifter and major instruments housed in a center cluster.

Above: Foreshadowing the Dodge Dakota convertible pickup truck, the Sidewinder concept incorporated the retro-inspired styling of the Ram pickup.

Below: The 1999 Dodge Charger was inspired by the fuselage body style of the 1968 model. But the iconic muscle car was reborn with a twist—four doors. Some of the styling cues from this concept can be seen on the current production Charger.

Above: Further evolving the ESX concept, the ESX2 was equipped with a second-generation hybrid powerplant as well as rear fender skirts to cut aerodynamic drag.

The 2000 ESX3 concept shows further refinement of the concept and hints at styling cues that would be used on the Intrepid-replacing Magnum.

## WHAT YOU SEE IS WHAT YOU GET

In 1989, the debut of the Viper R/T10 concept, was the first execution of "what you see is what you get" approach to show cars. The 400-horsepower, V-10-engine-powered roadster caused a sensation, and it was the first step in the Viper's product development process.

A year later, Dodge introduced the LRT concept, which stood for Lil Red Truck, a tribute to the '60s wheelstander and the '70s performance truck. The LRT concept helped build the case to go with a more radical approach on the next generation Dodge Ram pickup, which was slated to debut in 1994. The step fender look and cross-hair grille became the new face of the truck lineup.

At the other end of the spectrum, the Dodge Neon debuted in 1991, paving the way for the successor to the Dodge Shadow. This cute little concept sported round bug eyes that were incorporated in the production Neon. Those round headlamps and arched roof may look familiar—they predated the modern Volkswagen Beetle by eight years. In addition to sporting styling cues for the car that would be sold, the Neon was also used as a platform to showcase advanced technology that might not necessarily make it into production. In this case, it was a 2-stroke engine and power side doors that opened from the middle, eliminating the need for a B-pillar.

The 1992 Dodge EPIC minivan also blended the look of the next generation minivan with new technology in the form of electric power. EPIC stands for Electric Power Interurban Commuter. At the time, Tom Gale said, "Our platform team relationship now allows us to look at the many new and innovative engineering solutions in our concept vehicles as well as future design directions."

After taking a year off, Dodge returned in 1994 with four concepts, two production-based—the Viper GTS coupe and Ram VTS performance truck—and two that explored future designs. The most radical was the Neon-based Aviat, which

As Dodge prepares to introduce the rear-drive Magnum wagon, the Super8—a HEMI V-8-engine-powered family car—grafts Ram truck styling cues onto a traditional sedan.

The Super8 features coach-style "suicide" doors with no B-pillar, which make getting in and out of the cabin easier.

Inspired by the kid's scooter of the same name, the 2002 Dodge Razor is a bare-bones 2-seat sports coupe designed to appeal to a young audience.

featured a slick aerodynamic shape with scissor-style doors and outrigger-mounted rear wheels. Also making the rounds of the show circuit was the Venom, a rear-drive sport coupe powered by a 3.5-liter V-6 engine making 245 horsepower. It was part of an ongoing effort to develop a rear-drive platform for the Dodge car lineup, which was, except for the Viper, all front-drive.

The 1996 auto show star for Dodge was the ESX concept, which was a close representation of the second generation Intrepid front-drive sedan. The car featured a sleek, aerodynamic body, greater emphasis on the cab forward design philosophy that maximized cabin space and minimized the front overhang. The car also predicted the shift to hybrid power—it had a 75-horsepower, 3-cylinder diesel engine assisted by two 100-horsepower electric motors.

Dodge continued to look for a sporty rear-drive 2-seater to slot beneath the V-10 engined Viper as seen by the 1997 Copperhead concept. According to John Herlitz, who was vice president of design under Gale, "If Dodge Viper is credited for re-inventing the Shelby Cobra, then Dodge Copperhead should be credited for re-inventing a car in the tradition of the Austin Healey 3000." Powered by a 2.7-liter V-6 engine making 220 horsepower, the Copperhead had a 5-speed manual transmission and rear-wheel drive.

Two other concepts of note included the Sidewinder, a convertible Ram pickup powered by the Viper's V-10 engine, and the T-Rex, a 6x6 Ram that paid homage to the dual-rear axle trucks produced by Dodge during World War II. It's interesting to note that while the Sidewinder was never built, Chevrolet built a similar open-top retro pickup in 2003 called the SSR.

The 1998 lineup of show vehicles included the Big Red Truck, which played off the Ram pickup's semi rig–inspired looks in a heavy-duty variant, and an evolution of the Intrepid ESX concept. The ESX II featured faired-in rear wheels and was a so-called mild hybrid, which was less costly and more feasible for production than full hybrids. It was followed in 2000 by the ESX III, a further refined version of the concept.

Above: The 2004 Dodge Sling Shot is another youth-oriented vehicle, this time using a fuel efficient 100-horsepower, 3-cylinder engine that promised good mileage and plenty of thrills in a lightweight package.

Left: In looking for the next big thing beyond minivans, Dodge tried the 2003 Kahuna concept, which is a cross between a van and small crossover. Some of its styling elements are inspired by woody wagons and the VW Microbus.

Below: Perhaps the most outrageous concept to date was the 2003 Dodge Tomahawk, which essentially turned a Viper V-10 engine into a motorcycle.

Above: The 2006 Dodge Rampage explored the idea of a front-engine, front-drive pickup with a large cabin incorporating the Caravan's Stow 'n Go seating system, which allows the second-row seats to fold directly into the floor. The rear bulkhead could also be opened up to increase the cargo-carrying capacity of the box.

Below: In an effort to boost sales overseas, Dodge developed the Hornet minicar concept and introduced it at the Geneva Motor Show in 2006. The front-drive Hornet's squarish shape and fuel-efficient powertrain were targeted to international markets.

## RETRO RULES

As the new millennium approached, it seemed that automakers were looking backwards as much as they were looking forward. A number of the concepts were picking up on retro themes. Chief among these was the 1999 Dodge Charger, a 4-door interpretation of the 2-door classic, and the Dodge Power Wagon, which captured the macho look of the 1946 original.

In 2001, the Power Wagon evolved into the Power Box, a shape that foreshadowed the launch of the Dodge Durango SUV. A pure styling exercise that also joined the Power Box on the circuit was the Dodge Super8, a HEMI engine–powered family sedan best described as futuristic retro.

The Dodge Razor and the M80 were two concepts that were seriously considered for production in 2002 as part of an effort to appeal to the youth market. The Razor was a bare-bones 2-seat sport coupe with a front-mounted 250-horsepower I 4 engine and rear drive. It featured crank-up windows, no amenities like air conditioning or radio, and had a target price of $14,500. On the same score, the M80 was a small, bare-bones pickup truck with retro-inspired styling. It was equipped with a 210-horsepower 3.7-liter V-6 engine, 5-speed manual transmission, and 4x4 transfer case. While the M80 was seriously considered, the investment was deemed too steep versus the expected return.

Perhaps the oddest concept to come from Dodge in its history was the Tomahawk, a project championed by then Chrysler president Wolfgang Bernhard, who was brought over after the DaimlerChrysler merger. The Tomahawk was essentially a Viper V-10-engined motorcycle that featured dual front wheels. This monster was seen as more of a rolling art piece than a serious motorcycle. On a more realistic note, the 2003 Avenger concept was a precursor to the hatchback Caliber, while the whimsical Kahuna, a retro-inspired homage to the VW Microbus, explored a possible new minivan variant.

Dodge also toyed with the idea of getting into fun-to-drive minicars, as demonstrated by the 2-seat Slingshot. This 2004

The 1996 Intrepid ESX pointed directly to the second generation of the flagship sedan, which debuted two years later.

A companion concept to the 2002 Razor was the M80, a small, affordable pickup aimed at the youth market. The M80 was under serious consideration for production, but it was ultimately abandoned as too costly for the expected return.

show car had a lift-off roof panel and rear-mounted 1.3-liter 100-horsepower 3-cylinder engine.

A series of barely disguised production cars made the rounds for 2005–2006. This crop included the Caliber, which evolved from the Avenger concept; the Nitro, which was a sibling of the Jeep Liberty; and the Challenger, a retro homage to the original 1970 model.

The Dodge Rampage also debuted in 2006. The Rampage was a front-drive version of the Ram pickup, with cab-forward styling similar to the Dodge Maxxcab concept of 2000. Along with the Rampage came the Hornet, a front-drive subcompact designed for international markets. The Hornet featured suicide-style doors and was powered by a turbocharged 1.6-liter, 4-cylinder engine.

Still looking for that more affordable 2-seat alternative to the Viper, Dodge showed the 2007 Demon, a front-engine, rear-drive roadster designed to compete with the Mazda MX-5 Miata. Power came from a 172-horsepower 2.4-liter I4 engine, and in best Dodge tradition, it was a drivable prototype.

The last concept car in the traditional sense of an auto show dream car was the 2008 ZEO, which stood for Zero Emission Operation. This futuristic 2+2 sport wagon was envisioned as a performance EV with a range of 250 miles, featuring 268 horsepower delivered to the rear wheels via a single electric motor. The press materials claimed 0–60 acceleration of less than six seconds. Dodge followed up on the NEO a year later with the Dodge EV, which was essentially a Lotus-bodied 2-seat electric sports car with a reported range of 250 miles from its lithium ion batteries. The car was repainted from its original orange to yellow and called the Dodge EV Circuit when it made the auto show rounds in 2010.

Many of the show cars unveiled today are faithful representations of what the buyer can soon expect in the showroom. While Dodge may have been late to the dream car game, it has a rich history of providing some of the industry's most memorable concepts.

The 2007 Dodge Demon was designed as a challenger to the Mazda MX-5 Miata by using the 2.4-liter, 4-cylinder engine from the front-drive Neon in a rear-drive package.

In the Copperhead, Dodge tested the market in 1997 for a rear-drive sports car slotted beneath the Viper. The idea was to create a modern Austin-Healey.

# CHAPTER 9

# THE DODGE REBELLION

Though still based on the full-size Dodge chassis, the Dart continued to be downsized and took on a much smoother body with flowing character lines.

"To every action there is always an equal and opposite reaction."—Sir Isaac Newton

If the 1950s was an era of flamboyant fins and conformity, the 1960s was a time of big horsepower and a break from tradition. The former was all about exterior styling and keeping up with the Joneses, the latter was about what was under the hood and getting away from the Joneses.

The tenor of the times is best reflected in a mid-1960s call to consumers to "Join the Dodge Rebellion."

That rebellion was not unique to Dodge. While the early '60s saw the emergence of the compact car in reaction to the excesses of the previous decade, that didn't mean engines were being downsized. In fact, quite the opposite—displacement and horsepower grew exponentially.

And while the Greatest Generation propelled the industry to new heights in the 1950s, it would be the Baby Boomers who were getting their licenses in the 1960s that would take up the slack and soon be calling the shots on what kinds of cars Detroit should be building.

John Z. DeLorean and Pontiac are generally credited with creating the modern muscle car by putting a high performance V-8 in the intermediate sized Tempest and calling it a GTO, but it was Dodge that built on that formula and turned it into an art form by decade's end thanks to its class-leading "fuselage" design, scoring big-time roles in films like *Bullitt* and *Vanishing Point*, and generally tearing up drag strips and ovals in racing series ranging from NHRA to NASCAR.

During this period, the Dodge production car lineup is best described as small, medium, and large. Beginning in 1963, the Dart replaced the Lancer on the compact 111.0-inch wheelbase. The intermediate 119.0-inch platform consisted of 330, 440, and Polara models, while the large 122.0-inch remained the 880. The Coronet was added in 1965, and the Polara moved up to the 880's full-size platform and was joined by the Monaco.

## ENTER THE CHARGER

But it was the fastback Charger that debuted in 1966 that got the Dodge Rebellion rolling. While it may be viewed as a response to the Ford Mustang and Chevrolet Camaro, it was actually the success of the Plymouth Barracuda that provided the impetus for Dodge to make the Charger. Dodge dealers, seeing the success of their Plymouth cohorts, wanted a similar car, but Chrysler Chairman Lynn Townsend resisted. He insisted that if Dodge was going to build a sporty car, it would have to be an intermediate model and not be a knockoff of the Plymouth. The Plymouth was based on a compact car platform, the same approach used by Ford and Chevy for the Mustang and Camaro.

Above: Finally a true compact, the 1963 Dart, with its tidy body and Slant Six powerplant, was the quintessential economy car of the early 1960s.

Below: Retaining a 116-inch wheelbase, the 330 drops its Dart nameplate as that car makes the move to the intermediate platform. The 330 had clean lines and simple body shapes, though the front end was still laden with chrome.

The Charger's roots can be traced back to this 1964 concept, which was essentially a topless Polara coupe. This 2-seat show car retained the Polara's round headlights and bears little resemblance to the fastback that followed.

Above: A bulkhead divided the cockpit into driver and passenger areas, with the tachometer mounted high in the driver's field of vision. Note the toggle switches on the passenger side of the divider.

The original 1964 Charger concept toured the auto shows as an open car based on the Polara. Equipped with a 426-cubic-inch Wedge V-8 engine, the ruby red Charger sported a cut-down windshield and a Targa-inspired roll bar. Even though it looked slick, the division had a different idea in mind for the production car.

Engineers and designers used the Coronet coupe as a starting point. Thanks to its fastback shape, the 1966 Dodge Charger was, in a word, stunning. Designed by Carl Cameron, it featured hideaway headlamps (a first for Dodge) beneath its full width grille. Because it was on a larger platform than the Mustang and Camaro, it featured seating for four adult-sized passengers, and the rear buckets could be folded down to increase cargo space. Although the base engine was a 318 cubic-inch V-8 engine, the 425-horsepower 426 V-8 engine was an option, as was a 4-speed manual transmission.

Among the unique features of the four-passenger cabin were a full-length console that ran through the front and rear seating areas, and an instrument panel that featured a large tachometer nestled next to the speedometer. All of the instruments were lit using glowing electroluminescent material instead of conventional light bulbs.

The Charger launched on January 1, 1966, during the Rose Bowl telecast. It was heralded as "The Leader of the Dodge Rebellion." The Charger was an immediate hit both on the track and the street. Riding on a 111.0-inch wheelbase, the Charger's base price was $3,211, and 37,344 were built for 1966.

The fastback design of Charger immensely helped Dodge's competitiveness in NASCAR stock car racing. Although Dodge had enjoyed success in the series with its HEMI engine power, aerodynamics was becoming almost as great a factor as horsepower in finding speed. The shape almost proved to be too slick—drivers complained about lift, which was remedied with the use of a small lip spoiler on the rear deck. NASCAR, wanting to keep the stock in its stock car, insisted that the feature be used on its production cars. Dodge sent retrofit kits to dealers and adapted the spoiler standard to all 1967 models, making the Charger the first production car that used this aerodynamic device as standard equipment. Once fixed, the fastback Charger was just the ticket in NASCAR, where the car accounted for 18 wins in its first season and helped Dodge win the manufacturers' title.

The original body style of the Charger lasted for just two model years, 1966–1967. Second year sales dropped to 15,788, but a profound change in the car's look soon improved its fortunes.

Above: The 1965 Charger II was actually created after the production model's design had been finalized. The rear of the car is much longer than the street car.

Below: The Dodge Dart saw only minor changes to its grille for the 1964 model year.

Above: The front of the Charger II features exposed headlamps, while the '66 model that would follow had hideaway units.

# FUSELAGE STYLING TAKES OFF

**The 1968 makeover of the Charger ushered in a new era of automotive design.**

Working under Vice President of Design Elwood Engel, Richard Sias and Harvey Win created a modern classic in the revamped Charger. Embarking on a massive program to reshape all the cars in the line, Dodge adopted a new design philosophy it called "fuselage." The clean yet slab-sided look shared by all 1960s Dodge vehicles gave way to more rounded body sides that resembled the fuselage of jet aircraft. Chrome use was minimal, and in addition to the more rounded body sections, the Charger adopted a flying buttress C-pillar treatment and a rear deck that ended in a ducktail spoiler.

The hideaway headlamps remained, but the lamps that ran across the tail were replaced by twin round units. Further definition came from scallops in the hood and body sides to add some tension to the design. The wheelbase also grew to 117 inches, while the base price dropped to $3,014.

The car was sexy, cool, and menacing. And it was a runaway hit by comparison to the earlier models, finding more than 96,000 buyers in its first year.

The Charger could be equipped with a wide range of engines, from a Slant Six up through a 440-cubic-inch Magnum V-8 engine. The high performance Road/Track (R/T) package was offered for the first time and included the 440 Magnum, while the 426 HEMI engine was optional.

While the new car was beautiful, the changes wreaked havoc on the track—the flying buttresses and inset grille increased lift and slowed the race cars, so as a quick fix, Dodge built the Charger 500 with exposed headlamps, a grille from the Coronet, and a flush back window. Only 500 were built.

For 1969, the standard Charger was virtually unchanged except for a new split grille treatment and revamped taillamps—the standard dual round lights were replaced by two single units that featured a "racetrack" shape.

The fuselage-style body of the '68 Charger was a dramatic change from the original car's rather slab-sided look. Other classic cues include the inset grille, dual round taillights, and flying-buttress C-pillars.

The 1967 Dodge Polara 500 convertible epitomized the styling of the era—less chrome, cleaner lines, and thin pillars.

Minor cosmetic changes for 1969 included this split-front grille and twin "racetrack-style" taillamps that replaced the round units.

The 1969 model year would also be remembered from another star car, this one built for NASCAR. After the Charger 500 quick fix, Dodge decided to go all-out in developing a true aerodynamic edge over the competition. It found it with a pointed nose cap and high mounted rear wing, which NASCAR would only approve if these pieces were made available to the public. As a result, the Dodge Charger Daytona was born.

There are few, if any, mass production cars that look as outrageous as the Charger Daytona. With an 18-inch long nose and 23-inch high wing, the Daytona cost $3,993 (about $1,000 more than the base car), and only 505 were built out of total Charger production of just under 90,000 units in order to meet racing homologation requirements.

On the track, both the Daytona and its sister Plymouth SuperBird cracked the 200-miles-per-hour barrier at superspeedways. Although the Daytona competed for three years in NASCAR, Dodge sold its road-going supercar for just two model years. After 1970, Dodge left this very limited retail market to Plymouth.

The last year of the second-generation Charger debuted in 1970 and can be distinguished by its larger chrome surround on the front grille. Dodge sold about 49,000, but the Charger faced some cannibalization internally from the slightly smaller Challenger, a shapely 2-door variant of the Plymouth Barracuda. Riding on a 110-inch wheelbase, the Challenger could be equipped with a wide range of engines, from the Slant Six engine up through the 440 Magnum and 426 HEMI engines.

While Townsend originally didn't want Dodge competing with Plymouth in this segment, there had been a lot of horse-trading going on. After Plymouth introduced the Roadrunner (which used

Left: As in this photo documenting the assembly of the 1968 Dodge Charger, the process for building the car continued to evolve. While it still involved a moving assembly line, pits were introduced to make the job easier on the workers.

Below: The most dramatic step in the Charger's assembly process was the body drop onto the drivetrain.

Above: Fuselage styling appeared on the intermediate Coronet in 1969. The sheet metal wraps under the car and there is a subtle Coke-bottle shape to the body.

Below: Like the Coronet, the Polara also benefited from the shift to fuselage styling in 1969. This range-topping model rode on a full-size 122-inch wheelbase.

Above: The '69 model of the Dodge Dart, which had undergone a major makeover two years earlier, shares a family resemblance with the larger Coronet. The body features sharp character lines and clean sides. In place of the two-tone paint schemes that were all the rage in the 1950s, the late 1960s saw the increasing use of vinyl tops.

the same intermediate underpinnings as the Coronet and Charger), the dealers were clamoring for a sporty Dodge on the compact platform. Hoping to split the difference, Dodge built the Challenger on a wheelbase 2 inches longer than the 'Cuda. Part of this strategy was to position the Challenger against the more upscale Mercury Cougar, while the Barracuda would continue to go head-to-head with the Mustang.

Also designed by Carl Cameron, the Challenger actually used a grille treatment that he had penned for the original Charger variant that was envisioned to have turbine power. Even the Challenger name wasn't new—in 1959, a limited-edition model called the Silver Challenger was built, offered only as a 2-door coupe with a choice of I6 or V-8 engines in one exterior color—silver.

Unlike the larger coupe-only Charger, the Challenger was built in both coupe and convertible versions and sported unique features such as a pistol grip shifter. It was also the first Dodge to make use of injected-mold plastics for the interior trim.

In addition to the R/T package, Dodge also offered a sporty T/A package, which referred to the Challenger's entry in the Sport Car Club of America's Trans Am racing series. A car piloted by Sam Posey had several top three finishes, but Dodge ended the program after just one season. Just 2,399 street-going T/A models were produced.

## FAR OUT, MAN

A pop culture trend Dodge surfed during this period was its use of psychedelic colors with wordplay names—like Plum Crazy for purple, a green shade called Sub-Lime, an orange called Go Mango, and Top Banana yellow.

These were heady times for Dodge. In 1970, production reached an all-time high for one year of 836,155. But beneath this burst of creativity, booming sales, and model proliferation (in addition to Charger and Challenger, there were muscle car variants of the Dart, Coronet, and Polara like Swinger, Super Bee, and GTS), Dodge sales and marketing efforts had become the antithesis of the Dodge Brothers' early philosophy of simplicity. Sales soon plummeted, and Dodge had to not only put its own house in order, but also faced external challenges like fuel shortages, more stringent safety rules, and tightened emission requirements.

The 1960s may have been turbulent at times, but at least the Dodge Rebellion was a fun ride. But things were about to get serious.

Above: Lasting only three model years, the fuselage-shaped Charger migrated to the 2-door Coronet body in 1971 and featured a new grille surround and standard exposed headlights—hideaway units were optional.

Inset: There was no shortage of special performance models across the Dodge range, as this 1970 2-door Dodge Coronet Super Bee attests.

Below: Dodge introduced the Challenger in 1970 to compete more directly in the pony-car market. It had a slightly longer wheelbase than the Plymouth Barracuda and was positioned more upmarket against the Mercury Cougar.

# CHAPTER 10

# DODGE ON THE SILVER SCREEN

With its dark, menacing looks, a black Charger was the perfect choice for the hit men in Steve McQueen's 1968 movie *Bullitt*.

Frank Bullitt looks up and sees a black 1968 Dodge Charger in the rearview mirror of his Mustang. Thus begins a seminal cinematic chase scene on the streets of San Francisco in the Steve McQueen classic *Bullitt*.

Ultimately, the prey, Bullitt, becomes the hunter, turning the tables on the two hitmen who were in pursuit of the police lieutenant. It doesn't end well for the pair and their mount, as the Charger is consumed in a fiery crash.

Three years later, much the same fate awaits a white 1970 Dodge Challenger, driven by an ex-cop, Vietnam vet, and car transporter named Kowalski, who bet he could drive from Denver to San Francisco in less than a day. Barry Newman portrayed the driver, who was urged on by Super Soul, a blind DJ played by Cleavon Little in the film *Vanishing Point*. After eluding the cops for the better part of a weekend, the car and Kowalski meet an untimely end on the blades of two bulldozers blocking the road.

Both movies are emblematic of the turbulent times that encompassed the 60s. Anti-establishment and counter-culture attitudes held sway, and the non-conformist Frank Bullitt and rogue driver Kowalski were celebrated anti-heroes.

Both the Charger and Challenger bucked the established order of the day that mainly pitted GM against Ford in the sales race and on track. By striving to be different, Dodge was able to carve out a unique image thanks to the iconic American muscle cars it created.

Because the Dodge Charger and Challenger were celebrated bad boys in the movies, the division marketed cars as coming from the white-hatted Dodge Boys. Dodge also employed Joe Higgins, who portrayed a stereotypical Southern sheriff who announces "Boy, you're in a heap o' trouble," when pulling over a Dodge Challenger. Still, the underlying theme begun in the mid-60s called on consumers to "Join the Dodge Rebellion."

While *Bullitt* and *Vanishing Point* may come to mind when linking Dodge to pop culture, for the first half of its existence, the brand had a fairly low profile when it came to its presence in movies and song. The ubiquity of the Ford Model T made it a staple in early films, and perhaps the most famous song from the auto industry's infancy is "In My Merry Oldsmobile." There are no such praises in song for Dodge because, for the most part, the cars, while popular, were the automotive equivalent of sensible shoes. Aside from a series of mid-1930s print ads using movie stars like Eve Arden and Ginger Rogers to endorse Dodge, celebrities tended to gravitate to more upscale makes.

That began to change after the World War II, when styling and performance became a much bigger part of the Dodge identity. Sales and marketing moved quickly to promote the brand through entertainment.

The Dodge Monaco was popular among fleets, especially police departments. The big motor and the fact that it ran on regular gas sealed the deal for Elwood Blue to pick up a former Mount Prospect police car for the new Bluesmobile.

# PERFORMANCE BEGETS PUBLICITY

In 1956, Dodge introduced a pair of his and her cars for Roy Rogers and Dale Evans. The singers had been used for promotional appearances including the roll-off of the 1,000,001 Dodge in 1953 and with the 1954 Dodge Indy Pace Car. The '56 models included a Palomino Tan over Desert Sand Custom Royal convertible for Roy and a Custom Royal Lancer for Dale done up in Indian Turquoise over Desert Sand.

But it wasn't until the go-go 1960s that Dodge cars became the favorite heavy and hero in movies, television, and music.

It may have been the styling of cars like the Charger and Challenger that attracted the attention of directors, but more often than not, it was because of the performance. Max Balchowsky, a noted California road racer who prepped the 1968 Dodge Chargers and Ford Mustangs for *Bullitt*, said that while he did some engine tweaks to the Ford and beefed up the suspension for both cars to prepare them for the jumps, the two Chargers purchased at retail from a Glendale, California, dealer required no performance upgrades. He said that the Dodge cars could run circles around the Mustang.

In *Vanishing Point*, five 1970 Dodge Challengers were provided by the division, four equipped with 440-cubic-inch V-8 engines and one with a 383-cubic-inch. Again, the cars needed no modifications other than one jump car that was equipped with different shocks. The Challenger that is destroyed at the end of the movie is actually an engineless Camaro pulled by a chain into the bulldozers.

During the 1960s, Dodge cars were featured in songs like Jan & Dean's "Little Old Lady From Pasadena", who drove a superstock Dodge, as well as the 413 Super Stock Dodge Dart that is "shut down" in the Beach Boys song of the same name. Perhaps the most obscure musical reference to

Police versions of Dodge cars starred in many television and movie productions. In 1957, the CHP-liveried Coronet starred in the series *Highway Patrol.*

Dodge, however, can be found in a song by the Sacred Squall of Now, who released a recording called *Firedome* in 1995 that supposedly has a melody inspired by the V-8 engine's 1-8-4-3-6-5-7-2 firing order.

The best-known Dodge car of all, however, has to be the *General Lee*, a 1969 Charger that starred in the *Dukes of Hazzard* television show, which CBS aired for 145 episodes from 1979–1985. The series also spawned two made-for-TV movies, a theatrical release, and another TV movie that went direct to video. The show was actually based on a 1975 movie called *Moonrunners*, which starred James Mitchum (Robert Mitchum's son), who headlined another moonshiner flick, 1958's *Thunder Road*. In *Moonrunners*, the main character is Bobby Lee, who calls his Plymouth Fury *Traveler*, which was the name of General Robert E. Lee's horse. When adapted for television, a '69 Charger replaced the Fury, and though originally called *Traveler* as in the movie, the muscle car eventually became known as the *General Lee*.

Over the course of the series, somewhere between 250 and 320 *General Lees* were built and mostly destroyed as a result of the jumps and stunts. Noted for its orange paint scheme, Confederate Naval Flag décor, and welded shut doors that had Bo and Luke Duke climbing through the windows, the General Lee became a cultural icon in its own right, inspiring a song by Johnny Cash, "*The General Lee*", with the refrain "I'm a Charger, charging through the night…"

Though it's represented as a 1969 model, the producers altered a number of 1968 models to incorporate the later model year changes. Near the end of the series' run, as Chargers became harder to come by, the producers began using remote control models for some of the stunts, much to the chagrin of loyal *Dukes* fans.

The 1969 Dodge Charger R/T. The R/T has starred in numerous movies and television shows over the years—one of its most notable roles being the General Lee in *The Dukes of Hazzard*.

A modified Dodge Challenger is the daily driver of character Dominic Toretto, played by Vin Diesel, in *Fast & Furious 6*. Shown above is a 2013 Dodge Challenger R/T Blacktop.

While the Dodge Charger and Challenger have both developed a bit of anti-hero cachet over the years (see 1974's *Dirty Mary, Crazy Larry* starring Peter Fonda) and a 1974 Dodge Tradesman captured the essence of the customized van craze in 1977's *The Van*, the staple role for many Dodge products over the years has been the cop car.

From 1957–1959, the Coronets used in the TV show *Highway Patrol* were among the earliest appearances of Dodge cars on television. Dodge police cars continue to be staples in film and television. Goldie Hawn hijacked a Dodge Polara cop car in 1974's *The Sugarland Express*, which was also the first theatrical film of Steven Spielberg. Then there was the 1974 Dodge Monaco that Elwood Blues drives to pick up his brother Jake at the beginning of the 1980 hit, *The Blues Brothers*. Having traded their Cadillac for a microphone, Elwood shows up in a decommissioned Mt. Prospect police car boasting that it has "a cop motor, a 440-cubic-inch plant. It's got cop tires, cop suspension, cop shocks. It's a model made before catalytic converters so it'll run good on regular gas." Sadly, the *Bluesmobile* (one of 13 used in the film) completely falls apart near the end of the movie.

A concept car built by Dodge in 1984 and used as a pace car in the PPG/Indy Car World Series had a starring role in the 1986 movie, *The Wraith*, starring Charlie Sheen. The complicated plot involves the leader of a small town Arizona gang that intimidates victims into drag races where they lose their cars. That is until the Wraith rolls into town, a mysterious stranger in a black helmet and armored suit, menacing behind the wheel of a Dodge MS4 Turbo Interceptor to challenge the gang and avenge an unsolved murder. The MS4 had a mid-mounted twin-turbo 2.2-liter 4-cylinder engine and is said to have 440 horsepower, a top speed of 195 miles per hour, and 0–60 acceleration of 4.1 seconds.

Following the launch of the production version of the Viper in 1992, an NBC series also called *Viper* debuted in January 1994 but only lasted until April. Somewhat modeled after *Knightrider*, the crime fighting Viper could transform from a relatively stock looking R/T10 into a coupe called *Defender* that had a wide array of weapons and abilities. The show was cancelled in its first season, but it was later retooled and continued for three more seasons in syndication, from 1996 to 1999. The series also allowed Dodge and Chrysler to showcase other products like the Intrepid, Plymouth Prowler, as well as concept cars like the EPIC minivan.

Vintage Chargers continue to star in modern movies. *The Fast and the Furious* franchise, which began in 2001, featured a '70 model. In its fifth and sixth installments, the film series features the latest generation of rear-drive Dodge Chargers and Challengers.

So advanced is the styling of late-model Dodge vehicles that they have been featured in movies that are set in the future. Dodge Magnums were used as by the authorities in the 2005 picture, *The Island*. And Dodge teamed up with the SyFy channel to build a version of the new Charger that has a decided post-apocalyptic look in the series *Defiance*, alongside the new Dart. A video game that is based off the show also incorporates the Challenger in game play.

From classics to the latest models, Dodge plays its own unique role in entertainment and pop culture. It's not because Dodge is just another pretty face. Instead, it's proof of how tightly Dodge cars are woven into the fabric of American life.

The 1970 Dodge Challenger played as large a role as lead actor Barry Newman in the movie *Vanishing Point*.

# CHAPTER 11

# CHALLENGE AND CHANGE

Even the intermediate Dodge Polara was a huge car by today's standards. Two-door models were also quite popular during the era.

**America's muscle car era seemed to die overnight.**

It was the early 1970s. The 1973 OPEC (Organization of Petroleum Exporting Countries) embargo, a terrible economy, new safety and emission laws, and the enactment of such fuel savings measures as the 55-mile-per-hour speed limit and Corporate Average Fuel Economy standards created the perfect storm that doomed big cars and big horsepower.

But the transition to smaller, cleaner, safer, and more fuel-efficient cars was not a smooth one. The domestic automakers still had plenty of traditional body-on-frame full-size cars powered by V-8 engines in the pipeline, and Dodge was no exception. The smallest engine in the inventory was the in-line 198-cubic-inch Slant Six—the last Dodge car with a 4-cylinder powerplant was 1927's Fast Four.

With imports taking a larger share of the market, Dodge relied on the Dodge brand's global partnership with Mitsubishi to land the Colt for the 1971 model year. The Colt was a small subcompact imported from Japan in 2-door, 4-door, and wagon versions. The Colt was powered by a 100-horsepower, 1.6-liter 4-cylinder engine, and was the division's response to not only other imports like the Toyota Corolla and Datsun 510, but also homegrown 4-cylinder-powered competitors such as the Ford Pinto and Chevrolet Vega.

In addition to rounding out its lineup with the entry-level Colt, Dodge spent the first part of the 1970s weeding out redundant models and engine combinations. One of the first victims was the Challenger, which survived only four model years, getting the ax at the end of the '74 model year. The Charger was offered with a 6-cylinder engine for the first time in 1970, and was redesigned a year later, this time with exposed headlamps with optional hideaway units. To help trim the number of product offerings, Dodge dropped the 2-door coupes from the Coronet line and positioned the Charger as a replacement.

Another belt-tightening move was dropping the Polara after 1972. By 1975, Dodge's domestic car lineup consisted of the Dart, Coronet, Charger, and Monaco. The Monaco's biggest change was the shift from body-on-frame to unit body construction for the 1975 model year. Even though it was a major makeover, the Monaco was virtually as big as the car it replaced (the Polara) at a time when the demand was rising for downsized products. That year, Dodge produced only 335,942 cars, a half million less than just five years earlier. It was at that time 56-year-old Chrysler Chairman Lynn Townsend stepped down, replaced by his handpicked successor, John Riccardo.

In order to meet the new federal emission standards (which introduced unleaded fuel), engines were recalibrated to lower compression ratios with a corresponding drop in horsepower. The 440 Magnum of 1970 that was rated at 390 horses was pared back to just 215 by 1975.

The muscle car era carried on into the beginning of the 1970s, with lightweight cars like the Dart offering big-horsepower V-8 engines. One model was the 1971 Dart Demon, which rode on a shortened 108-inch wheelbase and was fitted with a 340-cubic-inch engine. The Demon name didn't stick; it was changed to Sport in 1973.

The Dart remained a perennial best-seller for Dodge through the middle of the 1970s. The logos of other models looked good too!

Doing yeoman's work during this transition period was the compact Dart, which actually saw its model count increase at a time when the large car stable was being scaled back. Offered in coupe and sedan versions, the Dart, riding on a 111-inch wheelbase, had three basic models: standard, custom, and the Swinger in 1970. A year later, a shorter wheelbase fastback coupe called the Demon joined the lineup, and buyers could choose from mild Slant Six versions all the way up to the 275-horsepower Demon 340—the successor to the GTS and Swinger 340 models. The Demon name stuck for only two model years and was redubbed the Sport in 1973. During this period, the Dart regularly topped 200,000 in annual sales.

As sales of the larger cars flagged, buyers who sought out the better fuel economy of compacts like the Dart also began demanding more amenities in their luxury cars. As a result, the Special Edition trim level was added, which featured vinyl roofs, plusher interiors, and power accessories. And there were other odd innovations, like the Convertriple—which featured fold down rear seats and a sliding steel sunroof. Why it was called a three-way convertible as the name implies when there are only *two* main features to the package remains a mystery.

This move to more upscale trim in the Dart line was a precursor to its replacement, the Dodge Aspen, which was introduced for the 1976 model year. Offered in 2-door, 4-door, and wagon body styles, the Aspen was larger (coupes rode on a 108.7-inch wheelbase, while the sedans and wagons had 112.7-inch wheelbases), and the interiors were more richly appointed than the Dart it replaced. It was offered in three trim levels—base, Custom, and SE—and could be equipped with the Slant Six or a choice of either a 318- or 360-cubic-inch V-8 engine.

The Aspen was one of the first cars designed using computer-aided engineering for the body, and was extensively tested in the wind tunnel to improve aerodynamics, boosting fuel economy in the process. Unfortunately, all early models were recalled due to premature rusting of the front fenders (a problem addressed by using galvanized steel fenders and plastic wheel well liners). The Aspen was noted for its good ride and bump isolation thanks to the Dodge brand's vaunted torsion bar suspension. The Aspen and its sister car, the Plymouth Volare, were rewarded by being named *Motor Trend* Car of the Year.

Having moved to and replaced the Coronet coupe body shell two years earlier, the 1973 Dodge Charger was well on its way to being reduced by fuel economy and emission standards. The biggest engine, a 440-cubic-inch V-8 engine, topped out at 280 horsepower.

# THE SWINGIN' SEVENTIES

In retrospect, there perhaps is no more schizophrenic era in the auto industry than the 1970s. After the muscle car explosion of the 1960s, the following decade had energy crises in both 1973 and 1979, and seemed to be ripe for small, practical, and fuel-efficient cars. Dodge sought to address those needs with the Colt and Dart, but it was also the era of the personal luxury coupe, and although these cars tended to be more intermediate rather than full-size cars, they didn't lack for creature comforts. More often than not, they were powered by V-8 engines—though by the end of the decade, most of these engines had been reduced by government regulations. In the 1960s, it seemed a bare-bones car equipped with a monster engine would suffice, but now with performance throttled back due to CAFE and emission standards, it was all about vinyl roofs, velour interiors, and opera windows.

These shifting tastes affected the Charger, which now shared its body shell with the Chrysler Cordoba. The new shell was a huge departure from the sleek fuselage styling of the second generation car—now, the Charger resembled a more formal 2-door coupe, and even sported an opera window. Instead of taking on muscle cars like the mighty GTO, it was positioned to compete with the Pontiac Grand Prix. But the Charger soldiered on through 1978, when it was marketed along with a twin called the Magnum, which differed only in its front fascia. Where the Charger sported round headlights, the Magnum had dual rectangular units beneath plastic lenses. These lights flanked a more modern grille with horizontal slats. By the next year, the Charger name was dropped entirely.

Above: The last gasp of the muscle car era is captured in this image of the 1974 Charger, which now had a chrome grille surround. The Dart and the Challenger were dropped the next model year.

Below: Another change in body style for the Charger came in 1975, when it shared sheet metal with the Chrysler Cordoba. Although it carried the Charger Daytona nameplate, the look is much more formal than the high-wing racer of just a few years earlier.

Above: The Dodge Monaco coupe embodied the shift away from performance to more luxury-oriented rides. In addition to hideaway headlights, the Monaco had a vinyl landau roof and opera windows.

Right: The compact Dart's replacement was the slightly larger Aspen, which was the first Dodge vehicle to use a transverse mounting of the company's vaunted torsion-bar suspension.

Design was not much of a priority during the 1970s, as demonstrated by the simple aesthetic of this 1976 Dodge Custom Coronet.

The latter half of the decade saw rapid changes to the Dodge lineup; the Monaco nameplate replaced the Coronet on the intermediate platform and the full-size car now known as the Royal Monaco. The Aspen sedan architecture was adapted to spawn the Diplomat, a more luxurious coupe and sedan designed to bridge the gap between Dodge's entry-level compact and the Monaco. The Diplomat was typical for its era—roomy and formal, with quad rectangular headlamps and an era-requisite vinyl top, with whitewall tires and wire wheel covers.

Truly large cars were becoming extinct. By 1979, the all-new R-body St. Regis, which not only rode on a downsized 118.5-inch wheelbase, but also shared the front end look of the Magnum, replaced both the Royal Monaco and the Monaco as the division's full-size 4-door sedan flagship.

The 1978 model year was also the last for the 400- and 440-cubic-inch V-8 engines, while the 360 carried on until 1981. The output of all these engines continued to fall. The last of the 440s made only 195 horsepower, while the 400-cubic-inch engine did have one version in the Charger that made 240 horsepower. The next year, the best the 360 could do was 195 horsepower. By 1983, the 318-cubic-inch V-8 engine hit its low point, producing only 130 horses.

The waning levels of performance also matched the waning involvement of Dodge in major motorsports. The heady days of the winged Charger Daytona were but a distant memory as the Magnum became the representative body style for the division in stock car racing. Kyle Petty won the last superspeedway race for Dodge in this era when he finished first at a Daytona ARCA race in 1979.

The Magnum itself was short-lived. It was renamed the Mirada for the '79 model year. The rechristening underscored a desire by Dodge to stress more of the personal luxury aspects of the car rather than performance.

Dodge continued to rely on Mitsubishi for its Colt economy car, and added a sporty coupe based on its Galant Lambda that marketed as the Challenger. Offered with a choice of either a 1.6- or 2.6-liter 4-cylinder engine, it remained in the lineup from 1978 to 1983. At the same time, the division was also preparing to launch a car that would point the way forward for virtually every Dodge vehicle, and involve a massive changeover from a past that relied on rear-wheel drive to a future that would be nearly all front-drive.

Below: Even the crisp lines of the Dart Swinger had begun to age by mid-decade. The large, impact-absorbing bumpers mandated in 1974 make the front end of the '76 model look heavy.

Bottom: In the mid-size segment, the rear-drive Diplomat was launched using a version of the Aspen platform. The Diplomat found a niche in police and fleet use.

Above: The 1978 Dodge Omni was the first domestic car to combine a transversely mounted engine with front-wheel drive. This efficient layout would be adapted for most of the cars in the Dodge line during the 1980s.

Below: In 1977, the Monaco lineup was split, with the Royal Monaco staying on a 121.5-inch wheelbase and the standard model replacing the Coronet on that car's intermediate wheelbase. Buyers had a choice of either a 400- or 440-cubic-inch engine, which made a respective 190 and 195 horsepower.

## GOES LIKE HELL

The 1978 Dodge Omni was a breakthrough car for the division on a number fronts—it was the first small transverse-engine, front-wheel drive car from a domestic manufacturer. The concept for the car was born in Europe through the Dodge brand's ties with Simca. Called an L-Body, the Omni in 4-door hatchback trim was in the same mold as the successful Volkswagen Golf (marketed in the United States as the Rabbit). In fact, Dodge relied on a 1.7-liter, 75-horsepower 4-cylinder engine from the German manufacturer to power early versions of the car until its own I-4 engine could be developed in-house. That engine—a 2.2-liter, 4-cylinder—was introduced in 1981. The Omni, which rode on a 99.2-inch wheelbase, was compact, fuel-efficient, and cost less than $4,000. Later, when Simca was sold to Peugeot, the car continued to be produced in Europe and sold as the Talbot Horizon—which was the same model name as the Plymouth variant.

In its first year, more than 80,000 Omni hatchbacks were built, and the line expanded in 1979 to include an angular 2-door hatch on a shorter 96.7-inch wheelbase called the O24 (which meant Omni 2-door, 4-cylinder).

The Omni line grew beyond just the two models, spawning an innovative front-drive pickup—sort of a mini Chevy El Camino—called the Dodge Rampage. The O24 coupe was later renamed the Charger, although its performance was a mere shadow of the classic muscle car. That's not to say that the Omni couldn't bring back old-school levels of performance; it took none other than Carroll Shelby of Ford Cobra fame to build a series of tuned cars for the company. The Omni GLH (which stands for Goes Like Hell) pumped out 146 horsepower from its turbocharged 2.2-liter 4-cylinder engine.

The Charger eventually gave way to the Dodge Magnum, another personal luxury coupe that had a bit more contemporary flare thanks to its rectangular headlamps beneath lens covers and its clean grille.

The Omni's diverse model lineup had the ability to appeal to buyers ranging from those on a tight budget (there were successful Miser and America series for the cost-conscious) up through those seeking spirited performance from the turbo GLH. This success was absolutely critical to Chrysler at the time, because it needed government-guaranteed loans to stay in business.

Although the company had weathered the first oil shock of the 1970s, its financial position became weaker as the decade progressed. Dodge production continued to bounce between 350,000 and 500,000 units, but by 1979, it had fallen again to 310,327. Riccardo reached out to former Ford President Lee Iacocca to become president and CEO in 1978—just a year after Iacocca had been fired by Henry Ford II—and who when asked why, famously said, "I just don't like him."

Iacocca, who was at the helm of the Ford division when it launched the groundbreaking Mustang, was reunited with one of his top engineers, Hal Sperlich, who preceded him to Chrysler. Together they would rewrite the book on how cars should be developed, creating a new approach of platform-sharing that is still in use to this day. And along the way, they would they would invent a new kind of vehicle that redefined family transportation.

But not yet. First, the company had to survive the threat of bankruptcy.

Based on the R platform, the St. Regis was the last traditional rear-drive, six-passenger, full-size V-8 engine family car sold by Dodge.

# CHAPTER 12

# IT'S A SMALL WORLD

The Dodge Stealth offered available AWD and a 320-horsepower Twin Turbo V-6 engine.

As the 1970s demonstrated, Dodge was able to leverage global contacts with both Mitsubishi and Volkswagen for cars and components necessary in its transition to more fuel-efficient front-drive vehicles.

## THE DODGE HEARD 'ROUND THE WORLD

While Dodge is considered a domestic brand, even back in its early days it had worldwide ambitions. Dodge never has had an international presence on the scale of Ford, but it has been successful in some overseas markets. But more important to the Dodge legacy is the way the division has benefited from connections to overseas automakers.

Dodge's participation in both World War I and II raised its profile abroad, but the earliest and strongest export market was Australia largely on the persistence of one Sydney A. Cheney,

From a fire-breathing V-8–engined American muscle car, the Challenger was downsized to a fuel-sipping 4-cylinder Japanese sport coupe inspired by Mitsubishi.

who had sold both Oldsmobile and Ford in New South Wales. After resigning from his job at an agency selling Ford vehicles, he travelled to Detroit hoping to secure a dealership from the Dodge Brothers. According to his autobiography, *From Horse to Horsepower*, his three-week wait earned him a job as Dodge's district sales representative for Australia, but more importantly, he was also awarded a dealership covering South Australia and the Western Darling District of New South Wales.

After receiving his first shipment of cars in late 1915, Cheney quickly sold out his allotment of seven vehicles, and within three years was outselling all the other dealers in his market. By 1917, Dodge was sending around 2,300 cars to Australia, but that summer, the government announced that it would no longer import car bodies. Cheney decided to import Dodge chassis and convinced H. J. and E. W. Holden (a leather goods firm which had been making interior and exterior car trim) to build complete bodies for him. Holden became a General Motors subsidiary in 1931. During that first year of the body embargo, Holden manufactured 5,000 bodies for Cheney, pushing Dodge Brothers' sales ahead of Ford's numbers.

Most of Dodge's overseas activity was in the British Commonwealth thanks to the company's expansion of production facilities in Windsor and Toronto, Canada. According to Charles Hyde's *The Dodge Brothers: The Men, The Motor Cars, and The Legacy*, a 1925 summary of exports reveals that 23,383 cars out of the 35,152 exported, were right-hand drive—a sign that they were headed to markets in the British Empire. Australia alone accounted for two-thirds of the 9,919 cars sent to Australasia, making that country the largest single export market for Dodge.

Even as Dodge cars were being sold globally, its approach differed from Ford, which had established manufacturing sites around the world. Instead, Dodge remains to this day primarily a North American manufacturer, sending its product from its base to selected global markets. After the acquisition by Chrysler, many of the exports from 1932 to 1959 were actually lower-cost Plymouth cars rebadged as Dodge Kingsways. And in an even odder twist, in 1960–1961, some Dodge Darts and Lancers were rebadged as DeSoto Diplomats and Rebels for export just prior to that division being shut down.

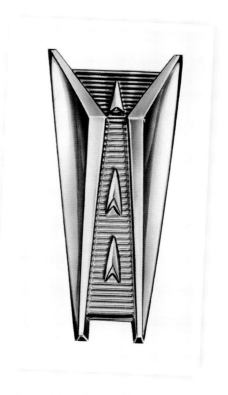

The emblem for the Dart from 1960 was as sharp as it was elegant.

Beyond its limited export program, Dodge's global ties through its parent Chrysler were pursued to strengthen the North American lineup. In 1971, Chrysler purchased a 15 percent share of Mitsubishi Heavy Industries, which led to the sale of that car's Galant model as the Dodge Colt. This was the first "captive import" in the corporation's stable.

The Mitsubishi connection lasted 40 years. In the early years, Dodge imported rebadged models like the Colt and later the Challenger (which was the Galant Lambda) as well as bringing in a succession of optional engines, both 2.6-liter 4-cylinder, and 3.0-liter V-6 engine powerplants used in a wide range of Dodge products. Mitsubishi also produced versions of its Starion sport coupes, which were rebadged Dodge and Plymouth Conquests, and sold from 1984–1985. Another vehicle in this vein was the Montero compact SUV, which Dodge called the Raider and sold from 1987–1989.

The last of these captive imports was the Dodge Stealth, a high-performance sport coupe offered in both front and all-wheel drive from 1991–1996. Built by Mitsubishi in Japan and sold by its subsidiary in the United States as the 3000GT, Dodge was able to have some input on the design, mainly the area of bolt-on body kits. The Stealth was powered by Mitsubishi's 3.0-liter V-6 engine in non-aspirated and turbo forms with output ranging from 164 to 320 horsepower.

**The 1998 Dodge Avenger.**

The relationship evolved further when Diamond Star Motors, a joint venture between Chrysler and Mitsubishi, established a Bloomington, Illinois, assembly plant in 1988 to build Galant sedans and new coupes, including the Dodge Avenger, Chrysler Sebring, Mitsubishi Eclipse, and Eagle Talon. Three years later, Mitsubishi bought out the Chrysler interest in the plant but continued to build cars for Dodge, Chrysler, and Eagle.

The Avenger, introduced in 1995, rode on a 103-inch wheelbase and replaced the sporty Daytona coupe, which was discontinued in 1993. The new 2-door offered a choice of either a 2.0-liter 4-cylinder or 2.5-liter V-6 engine. In 2000, it was redesigned and rebadged the Stratus coupe. Remaining on the Mitsubishi platform upon which it was based, it didn't share any of the components of the Stratus sedan. The coupe ceased production in 2005.

Following the merger of DaimlerChrysler, the stake in Mitsubishi was eventually sold off in 2005, and the Diamond Star plant no longer produced cars for Dodge.

While Mitsubishi figured prominently by providing both engines and complete cars to Dodge, it wasn't the only foreign manufacturer to do so. The 1987 acquisition of AMC/Jeep by Chrysler from Renault brought a new Canadian assembly plant, Brampton, into the fold. At the time, it was producing a new full-size front-drive sedan intended to be marketed as the Renault Premier. The car was subsequently sold under the new Eagle brand created by Chrysler to market cars previously sold as Renaults.

The new sedan was designed by famed Italian designer Giorgetto Giugiaro. It featured longitudinal mounting of the engine and a choice of two engines: either a 2.5-liter 4-cylinder engine developed by AMC, or an optional 3.0-liter V-6 engine developed by a consortium of Peugeot-Renault-Volvo, the PRV V-6 engine, the same engine in the ill-fated DeLorean.

A later version of the Colt was the Vista, a tall wagon that was positioned as a type of "mini" minivan.

The new Dodge Dart was developed in just 18 months and has enabled Dodge to return to the forefront of the compact car game. Above is the 2013 model.

Part of the agreement with Renault was a contract to provide a fixed number of the PRV drivetrains. When it became apparent that the fledgling Eagle division did not have a big enough dealer body or established brand reputation to hit the sales objective required by the contract, Chrysler decided to sell a version of the car through the Dodge network as the Monaco. The Monaco differed from the Premier in its grille treatment and trim, and it was offered only in a V-6 engine. Launched in 1990, it was sold through 1992 as a replacement to the rear-drive Diplomat. It wasn't the first time that an engine with French lineage had appeared in a Dodge product— Peugeot provided a 1.6-liter 4-cylinder engine for the Dodge Omni from 1983 to 1986.

The Monaco, while not highly successful, was an important link in Dodge history, for its architecture and assembly plant served as the basis for the groundbreaking cab-forward Intrepid to follow.

While the Monaco was part of Dodge's French connection, there was also a bit of British auto legacy as a result of Chrysler's purchase of the Rootes Group in 1967. Rootes owned a brand called Hillman, which produced a small, rear-drive 4-cylinder-powered model riding on a 98-inch wheelbase called the Hillman Avenger. The Hillman Avenger was available in 2-door, 4-door, and wagon configurations, and sold as the Dodge Avenger in South Africa. In Brazil and Argentina, it was sold as the Dodge 1500, 1800, and later as the Polara. A pickup version of the Dodge 1500 was also sold in Uruguay.

While Dodge was selling the Mitsubishi-built Colt, the Plymouth was selling the Hillman in the United States as a Cricket. And showing the global nature of tie-ups throughout the auto industry's history, VW also sold the 1500 in Argentina, later providing 1.7-liter 4-cylinder engines for the Dodge Omni. In 1978, when Chrysler Europe declared bankruptcy, Rootes and Simca were sold to Peugeot and the Dodge branding of Hillmans ceased.

The overseas influence on Dodge products continued through the DaimlerChrysler era, most noticeably with the introduction of the rear-drive LX platform used to develop the Magnum, Charger, and Challenger. This successor to the front-drive LH incorporated the suspension layout and components from the Mercedes-Benz E-Class. Although the DaimlerChrysler marriage was troubled, the LX demonstrated that there were some synergies to be had from this cross-Atlantic alliance.

The Dodge Sprinter was another product of this era. Originally introduced in Europe as a Mercedes-Benz van in 1995, the Sprinter debuted in the United States in 2001 as the Freightliner, an American heavy-duty truck maker owned by Daimler-Benz. With the demise of the third–generation B-van in 2003, Dodge replaced its full-size entry in both the commercial and retail markets with the Sprinter, which could be outfitted as a work truck, passenger van, or RV. The Sprinter was totally redesigned for the 2007 model year, and three years later, the contract between Dodge and Daimler to market the vehicle expired, and sales were taken over by Mercedes-Benz.

## NEW CARS, NEW MARKETS

With the advent of the Fiat connection, Dodge is poised to further benefit from the expertise of its overseas partner in a way that will not only speed up product development, but also to ensure that the division remains on the cutting edge of technology. The Dart is the first evidence of this approach. Developed in 18 months using a variation of Alfa Romeo's Giulietta platform called the Compact U.S. Wide (CUSW), the Dart has enabled Dodge to get back into the compact car game quickly with a credible entry that features leading-edge technology like Fiat's patented MultiAir® variable valve technology.

Conversely, the Dodge Journey crossover is finding new markets as the Fiat Freemont in Europe, the Dodge JC in Japan, and the Dodge JCUV in China. The Journey, which is assembled in Toluca, Mexico, has also made inroads in Australia, where Dodge's overseas adventure began. All but given up for dead Down Under, the introduction of the Journey crossover with the Dodge nameplate is part of a plan to expand the portfolio in that country. The Journey was first launched in 2008 with a standard 2.7-liter V-6 engine and an optional 2.0-liter 4-cylinder turbodiesel with a dual clutch transmission. The venerable SUV is positioned as a 7-seat upscale crossover. The fact that Dodge can continue to survive and thrive in the far corners of the world pays tribute to the vision of John and Horace Dodge, as well as the persistence of Sydney A. Cheney.

# CHAPTER 13

# THE K-CAR REVOLUTION

The untimely passing of the Dodge brothers denied the company their vision and talent. Fortunately, the Dodge company had always been about the product and not personalities.

Still, from time to time, several larger-than-life personalities figure in the Dodge story. One of them was Walter P. Chrysler. The other was Lee Iacocca.

It was precisely the family's influence over Ford that led Iacocca to Chrysler's doorstep. With his hands firmly on the reins, Iacocca was prepared to make a profound impact on Chrysler and Dodge during its darkest hours.

Trained as an engineer, Iacocca's early career at Ford included stints in regional sales and marketing, and his sense of picking product winners was second to none. He was a natural

The Aries was introduced as a complete family of vehicles. In addition to the wagon and sedan pictured here, the car was also available as a 2-door coupe.

Above: The 1978 Dodge Omni was the division's first front-drive car and set the stage for the K-Car revolution that would follow.

Below: The first vehicle based on the K-Car platform was the Dodge Aries. Because of the transverse engine and front-drive layout, it offered mid-size roominess in a compact package.

pitchman who knew how to work the halls of politics. He would need all these skills to bring the company back from the brink of bankruptcy.

Bringing the force of his personality to bear, Iacocca successfully persuaded the government to guarantee a $1.5 billion loan—the largest government loan at the time, ever. It was the money Chrysler needed, however, to finance the turnaround. One of the conditions of the financial package was that John Riccardo would have to step down, putting Iacocca in charge as chairman. What followed was a painful restructuring of the company that led to massive layoffs and plant closings, including the shuttering of Dodge Main in 1980.

## REVOLUTION

Dodge Main had been the one constant in the 70-year history that predated Dodge Brothers' first car. Once a showplace of the latest in auto manufacturing technology and vertical integration, it had become an outdated, inefficient multi-story and multi-building complex in which it was difficult for even industry insiders (much less casual observers) to follow the assembly line. In 1981, the complex was sold for $1 and leveled as part of deal to help General Motors build its new Detroit-Hamtramck assembly plant, which was to be a showcase of automation. That plant ended up employing only a fraction of the workers of Dodge Main and had its own problems, including a breakdown in the automation.

The automated robots were reportedly painting each other.

Splatter-painted robots or not, the closing of Dodge Main was a clear sign that it was not business as usual. Iacocca had promised a New Chrysler—a new car company with more efficient manufacturing—and he needed a product plan that would shift the model mix away from large, rear-wheel-drive sedans that weren't selling to compact front-drive cars that were.

Building on what had been learned in creating the front-drive L-body Omni, the company embarked on a program to develop a front-drive replacement for the Aspen. This model, called the Aries (the Zodiac sign for Ram) was based on an all-new architecture known as the K-Car.

Introduced in 1981, the Aries rode on a 99.6-inch wheelbase and came in 2-door, 4-door, and wagon versions. It featured front-wheel drive with a transverse-mounted engine and choice of a 3-speed automatic or 4-speed manual transaxle. The front-wheel drive layout provided tremendous advantages in packaging, giving the compact Aries nearly the same interior space as most intermediates. The cars were much lighter than similar size rear-drive cars, tipping the scales at less than 2,400 pounds. Aries offered two 4-cylinder engines: either an in-house built 2.2-liter unit, or a Mitsubishi-supplied 2.6-liter unit. Fuel economy soared—the base car carried an EPA rating of 27 miles per gallon in the city and 41 miles per gallon on the highway.

The Aries was more than two feet shorter than the Aspen it replaced, and it featured state of the art technology such as MacPherson strut front suspension and rack-and-pinion steering. It also represented a switch in the marketing approach—the internal engineering letter designation, K, became an integral part of the sales campaign. It allowed Chrysler to sell both the Dodge Aries and Plymouth Reliant under one banner—K-Car—and provided cross-promotional opportunities such as working with K-Mart.

Chrysler, which had lost $2 billion in 1980 and was on the brink of shutting its doors, sold over 300,000 K-Cars. By 1983, the company that had asked the government for $1.5 billion was back in the black.

Above: As the front-drive K-Car revolution spread, older rear-drive models like the Mirada died out. This 1982 Mirada, with a fake convertible top, was the penultimate model year. The rear-drive Diplomat soldiered on, however, primarily used as a fleet vehicle.

Inset: While its dimensions were virtually identical to the Aries, the Dodge 400 introduced in 1982 offered more luxurious trim. This 2-door sports a vinyl roof and opera window as well as a plusher interior than the standard Aries.

## THE RETURN OF A CLASSIC

The K-Car platform proved to be flexible and cost-efficient for Chrysler, and spawned additional models. In 1982, Chrysler introduced the more luxurious 400, which offered not only 2-door coupe and 4-door sedan versions, but also the first convertible in the Dodge lineup since the 1971 Challenger. The convertible was originally built by an outside supplier (Cars & Concepts), but proved so successful that it eventually moved in-house alongside sedan and coupe assembly.

Top: Dodge relied on racing great Carroll Shelby to infuse some excitement into the division's front-drive offerings with models like this Shelby Charger

Inset: A 4-door econobox was an unlikely candidate to be a performance-car icon, but Carroll Shelby worked his magic on the Omni to produce the GLH, a designation that stood for "Goes Like Hell."

The 400 was called the Super-K, though it basically was the same as the Aries in mechanical specification and dimension. But Dodge was able to position it above the standard Aries by offering plusher interiors, padded vinyl roofs, and more sound insulation to give it a luxury car feel.

About this time, Dodge phased out its largest car, the 118.5-inch wheelbase St. Regis. The only rear-drive cars left in the lineup were the Mirada personal luxury coupe and the Diplomat 4-door sedan. Mirada was discontinued, but the Diplomat remained in production, primarily to serve police, taxi, and other fleet car markets.

Using the K platform as a building block, Dodge added a longer sedan called the 600 to the lineup in 1983. Internally designated as the E-body, it stretched the wheelbase to 103.1 inches. A year later, a turbocharged 2.2-liter 4-cylinder engine making 142 horsepower was added. At the same time, the shorter 400 coupe and convertible (now on 100.3-inch wheelbases) became part of 600 model range.

The 1984 model year is also remembered for the return of two legendary names—the Charger, which was essentially a renamed Omni O24 sport coupe, and the Daytona, which was a fastback 2-door front-drive coupe on a modified 97-inch K-Car platform. The lightweight Daytona, when fitted with the 142-horsepower 2.2-liter engine in the Turbo Z model, offered 0–60 acceleration in fewer than nine seconds, which was quite good for the times.

The Daytona also was the first Dodge built in a new assembly plant in suburban Sterling Heights, which added much needed modern car building capacity in the wake of the Dodge

Main closure. Chrysler originally constructed Sterling Heights in 1953 to build missiles for the military but sold the property to Volkswagen in 1980. The German automaker, which had one U.S. assembly plant in Pennsylvania, wanted to add a second plant in Michigan. But the same downturn in the economy that nearly destroyed Chrysler also hit VW hard, and VW sold the facility back to Chrysler in 1983.

The Daytona was a venerable vehicle. It became a mainstay in the lineup for a decade, with special Shelby models; a Lotus-derived 224-horsepower, 4-cylinder turbo; and even a V-6 engine wedged beneath its hood. A special IROC package was even offered, reflecting the car's use for several seasons in the International Race of Champions series; the IROC series pitted the top stars in road racing and NASCAR against each other on ovals and road courses.

So successful was the K-Car model that Dodge resurrected a classic nameplate—the Lancer. This stylish 4-door hatchback was internally designated the H-Body, and the Lancer was meant to be to Dodge sedans what the Daytona was to the standard K coupes. Essentially, it was a performance-oriented family car, but when equipped with the turbocharged 2.2-liter engine, the Lancer was capable of turning in 0–60 times similar to that of the Daytona Turbo Z.

Such was the beauty of the K-Car program that its large economy of scale allowed Dodge to manufacture cars ranging from the entry-level Aries, through plush mid-size cars that offered full-size comfort in the 600, as well as performance-oriented machines like the Daytona and Lancer. But even those vehicles were not the stars of the era; that honor would go to a less aerodynamic—but no less revolutionary—vehicle all its own.

Above: Looking to Europe for inspiration, the Dodge Lancer was a mid-size 4-door hatchback that valued spirited handling over a plush ride.

Below: Based on the G-Car platform, the Daytona became Dodge's premiere domestically produced sports coupe in the lineup.

Above: The Omni-based Charger was replaced by the Shadow, a 2- and 4-door hatch with more of a traditional sedan appearance.

Below: Below: The last car built off the K-Car architecture was the C-body Dodge Dynasty, positioned as the full-size family car in the line. The front-drive sedan featured seating for six with front and rear bench seating and was offered with a choice of 4- or 6-cylinder engine power.

# THE GAME CHANGER

The seminal vehicle of this period was the Dodge Caravan. It was the first front-drive production minivan, and it revolutionized family transportation.

There are many stories (and fathers) of the minivan. Some say Chrysler was working on a rear-drive minivan in the early 1970s, but the idea was shelved because GM and Ford were not building them. Hal Sperlich, who at Ford had proposed doing a front-drive vehicle he called the Mini-Max and was turned down, is credited with championing the minivan idea at Chrysler about the time Iacocca joined the company. The big change that enabled the development of the van at Chrysler was the switchover to front-drive with Omni and Aries.

The larger Aries K-Car platform was ideally suited as the jumping off point for the minivan. While many of the K's components were used on the Caravan, the official designation in-house for the vehicle was T-115. The layout was simple—a 4-cylinder transversely mounted engine drove the front wheels. The suspension was front MacPherson strut with a torsion beam rear axle. The minivan, thanks to the front-wheel drive, was small enough to fit in a garage, yet the seating position was upright and tall, giving the driver a command-of-the-road feeling. The roomy cabin had a flat floor, two front bucket seats, and second-row 2-passenger bench offset to the driver's side, allowing for walk-through access front to rear. The original minivans also featured a sliding door for the rear passengers, but only one was implemented. Ostensibly this was for safety reasons, but it also reduced cost and complexity in the build process.

Offered with the 2.2-liter 4-cylinder engine standard and the Mitsubishi 2.6-liter I4 engine as an option, the Caravan debuted as a 1984 model. It rode on a 112-inch wheelbase, could carry up to seven passengers, and yet was the same overall length as the Aries station wagon. This minivan also had the advantage of removable seats, allowing it to carry several 4x8 sheets of plywood or other sizable cargo.

The minivan was an unqualified success, creating a vast new market segment where none had existed before. Dubbed the Magic Wagon, Dodge used famed magician Doug Henning in its advertising for the Caravan.

A longer version of the Caravan was introduced in 1987, riding on a 119.1-inch wheelbase. The Grand Caravan offered additional storage behind the third-row seats, and it was fitted with more upscale amenities. Midway through the model year came engine changes that replaced the base 2.2-liter with a Chrysler-built 2.5-liter I4-cylinder engine, and the 2.6 from Mitsubishi was replaced by a 3.0-liter V-6 engine, also from Dodge's Japanese partner. By 1989, a 3.3-liter V-6 engine—the first all-new engine developed in-house since the 2.2-liter 4-cylinder engine—became the top engine.

In addition to the family haulers, Dodge introduced the Mini Ram Van (a commercial variant of the Caravan) along with a camper option, which was offered from 1984–1986.

Below: Hoping to offer a driving experience and package to rival European competitors, Dodge offered the Lancer, a 4-door hatchback with sedan styling that offered turbocharged performance models.

The Spirit R/T was introduced in 1991 and was equipped with a 224-horsepower Turbo III engine.

## IACOCCA FOR PRESIDENT

The success of the minivan, along with the strong sales of all the other K-Car variants, changed Chrysler's fortunes almost overnight.

Enthusiastic consumers thought Iacocca could do anything (up to and including running for president). Chrysler, flush with cash, went on a buying binge.

First, Iacocca engineered the acquisition of business jet maker Gulfstream. Then Lamborghini. Then American Motors, in 1987. On a historical note, it's ironic that Iacocca wanted AMC primarily for its Jeep brand, which was previously owned by Willys-Overland, a company that Walter Chrysler was looking to buy when he instead opted for Dodge because of its factory and dealer body. Now Jeep brand vehicles, still built in the old Willys-Overland plant in Toledo, would finally become affiliated with the Dodge brand.

Profits also flowed back into the business to increase model offerings. The aging Omni was slated to be replaced in 1987 by the Shadow, a slightly smaller 2- and 4-door hatchback heavily inspired by the Lancer design. The Omni continued to sell well, however, and was manufactured through the 1990 model year, marketed primarily as a value-oriented entry-level econobox. The 2-door Charger, however, was dropped in favor of the all-new Shadow.

The same strategy also applied to the Aries, and its replacement, the Spirit. Significantly upgraded over the original K-Car platform, the Spirit (called the A-Body internally), debuted in 1989. This new mid-size entry was offered with a choice of 4- or 6-cylinder powerplants, and

The Dodge Caravan proved to be a flexible package. A cargo version was marketed as the Mini Ram van.

it was longer and roomier than the K-Car it replaced. However, rather than immediately kill the Aries, this original K lived on as the value-priced Aries America model until the 1991 model year.

The only other addition to the Dodge stable during this period was the top-of-the-line Dynasty sedan, the last true heir to the K-Car legacy. Riding on a wheelbase stretched to 104.3 inches, the so-called C-Body was launched as a 1988 model. The Dynasty was a traditional American family sedan, from its column shift automatic to its front and rear bench seats that could accommodate six passengers. Even with its velour interior and padded landau vinyl roof, its K-Car origins were easily detected in its roomy styling. And true to all K models, the base engine was a 2.5-liter 4-cylinder engine, although a V-6 engine was an option.

The Dynasty was a fitting capstone on the K-Car revolution, a revolution that had spawned perhaps the widest range of vehicles ever offered from a common architecture. Because of this product onslaught in the 1980s, Dodge was able to lift itself from eighth place among nameplate sales to sixth overall, climbing back up over the half-million mark by 1988.

There's no doubt that the turnaround in Dodge's fortunes in the 1980s were clearly born from the desperate measures needed to stave off bankruptcy. Unfortunately, when times are flush, some of that razor-sharp focus of the past is lost. It wouldn't be long before what went up was about to come down—hard. Dodge would be facing more troubled times ahead but would find its way forward this time with a car that would be the very antithesis of the K-Car, Dodge's fortune-changing every-vehicle of the '80s.

Above: One of the innovative features of the original 1984 Dodge Caravan was the ability to pass through the vehicle from the front row to the third, thanks to a second row bench that was offset to the driver's side.

Below: The face of the Daytona continued to be updated, and by 1992 it had flush headlamps instead of the original dual rectangular units.

# CHAPTER 14

# SAFETY PROVES
# TO BE A SELLING POINT

Adjusted for inflation, the 1914 Dodge cost $785. Today, it would retail at over $18,000 and fail to meet any of the safety requirements for new cars.

When John and Horace Dodge built their first car, dependability and quality topped the list of attributes they wanted associated with their product. While safety was not the selling point that it is today, the Dodge Brothers approach of continuously improving the product has played a major role in incorporating safety advances in cars and trucks carrying the Dodge nameplate.

The fact that the Dodges insisted that their first car have a steel body and later models pioneered unit-body construction figures in later developments such as computer-aided engineering to develop crumple zones, thereby reducing the severity of vehicle impacts upon the occupants.

But in those early years, the word *safety* is hardly used—the emphasis was on stressing the ease of operation and durability of the product at a time when the automobile had to prove itself as a viable means of personal transportation.

It wasn't until the Walter P. Chrysler era that safety was formally recognized (although it can be said the adoption of such features as power hydraulic brakes in 1932, which made driving easier, also contributed to making the cars safer thanks to the technology's greater stopping power). Of course, much of those early product improvements, from electric starters to electric lights, can be looked upon as making motoring safer.

But passive safety got its first boost with the 1937 Dodge cars, which along with their Chrysler, Imperial, DeSoto, and Plymouth counterparts, benefited from a wide range of improvements designed to protect passengers. Among the advancements were a new flush dash design, which featured padding and recessed control knobs along with additional padding on the rear seats and armrests. The door handles were also curved inward to prevent them from snagging coat sleeves when getting in and out of the car.

## SAFETY FIRST

It wasn't until nearly 30 years later that automotive safety was recognized as being important enough to warrant federal regulation. And it was a time when car buyers were also becoming interested in a vehicle's safety when considering their next purchase.

Landmark legislation in 1966 established new requirements mandating such features as lap belts, padded dashboards,

shatterproof glass, headrests, and energy-absorbing steering wheels. The laws also established the National Highway Safety Bureau, forerunner of today's National Highway Traffic Safety Administration, which sets crash standards and requires safety equipment such as air bags.

During the '60s and '70s, Dodge, like all other automakers, scrambled to keep up with the rapidly changing regulatory environment as a flood of emission control, fuel economy, and safety regulations washed over the industry at a time of economic upheaval. Chrysler's Huntsville electronics division (one of its greatest assets, with clients including the space program and even the military) became a leader in developing the on-board electronics

The interior of the 1930 Dodge Eight shows how rudimentary and dangerous early cars were. There's no collapsible steering column, the dash is metal with protruding knobs, and there are no seatbelts.

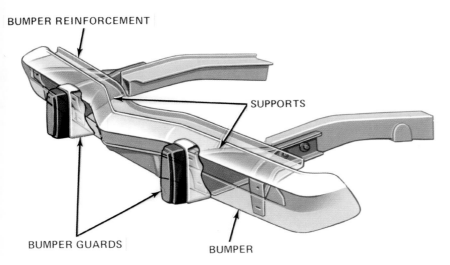

BUMPER REINFORCEMENT

SUPPORTS

BUMPER GUARDS

BUMPER

In order to meet new federal regulations, Dodge developed this bumper system in 1973 to enable the car to absorb a 5-mile-per-hour impact without sustaining damage.

that would enable Dodge products to not only meet these standards, but to exceed them.

Rival car companies also made advances in addressing these regulatory challenges, and many companies even shared technology, most notably GM's invention of the catalytic converter. The catalytic converter was a huge step forward for the automotive industry, as it allowed cars to run on unleaded gas in order to comply with stricter clean air standards. And while GM first offered air bags as an option in 1974, the devices were too expensive and complicated for use on mass-market models. Most manufacturers adopted passive automatic seatbelts to meet the federal standards for occupant protection, and like GM, offered air bags only as options on upscale models. But in 1988, Chrysler offered a standard driver's side air bag in six of its volume model lines (including those of Dodge), and a year later, made the devices standard across the board, becoming the first major manufacturer to do so, thanks in part to electronic advancements it had developed.

Safety has also been in the forefront of the minivan story. Since the Dodge Caravan was purpose-built for the duty of family transportation, occupant safety ranked high on the list of attributes sought by buyers. In fact, it is often the prime consideration ranking higher than styling or performance.

Because children are the reason most people buy a minivan in the first place, great care was taken in the design of the vehicle to ensure the safety of this precious cargo. Among the innovations that were introduced first on minivans includes child safety locks on the sliding door in 1991, and the integrated child safety seat for the 1992 model year.

While the federal government was the impetus behind most of the safety efforts in the 1970s and early '80s, since then, carmakers have taken the lead, offering such active safety features as stability control, tire low pressure warning systems, back-up cameras, parking sensors, blind spot detection, adaptive cruise control, and lane departure warning systems long before such technology is required by law. New systems that warn of crashes and assist with braking are also being adopted across the board.

Dodge and Chrysler were the first in the industry to offer driver's-side air bags as standard equipment.

Left: This close-up shows the child-safety locks engineered for the sliding doors on the 1991 Caravan.

Right: This graphic shows the placement of an accelerometer, which is used in determining the force of a crash and whether the air bag needs to be deployed.

Below: This 1937 seven-passenger Dodge sedan incorporated a number of safety features, including a padded dash with recessed controls.

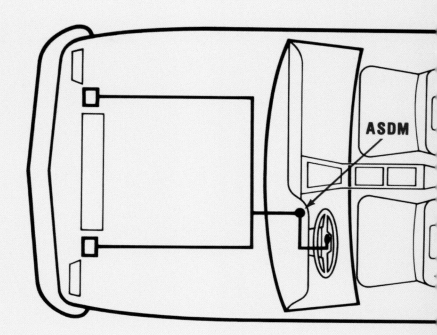

ASDM

Right: Another innovation pioneered by Dodge and Chrysler in 1992 was the integrated child-safety seat used in the second-row bench on minivans.

Below: Introduced with a base price of about $16,000, the 2013 Dodge Dart offered 10 air bags and a host of standard safety and security features that have enabled it to receive the highest rating in the Insurance Institute for Highway Safety's 40-mile-per-hour crash test.

# A CENTURY OF PROGRESS

Evidence of how far Dodge has come on safety can be seen in a comparison of the entry-level 2013 Dodge Dart versus the first Dodge car introduced in 1914. Today's Dart is the equivalent of the solid, dependable, and affordable car sold by Dodge Brothers a century ago. Back then, that first Dodge cost $785, which when adjusted for inflation, would cost $18,055 a century later. When the Dart was introduced for the 2013 model year, it had a base price of $15,995. Not only is the Dart more powerful and has a host of creature comforts undreamed of in John and Horace Dodge's time, but it also comes with more than 60 standard and optional safety features.

The Dart's safety and security story begins with the high-tech, computer-designed steel body, something that the Dodge brothers would surely appreciate. High-strength steel makes up 68 percent of this unit body. In addition, the Dart also employs aluminum in key crumple zones. This combination results in a rigid safety cell able to absorb crash impacts, minimizing the transmission of these forces to the passenger compartment. Following tests that included a 40-mile per hour frontal crash, the Insurance Institute for Highway Safety (IIHS) rated the Dart as a Top Safety Pick, an honor also shared by much larger vehicles in the Journey, Grand Caravan, and Durango.

Providing additional protection is the supplemental restraint system that consists of 10 air bags. The front passengers are protected by two-stage chest and kneebags, as well as seat-mounted thorax and pelvic bags for side impacts. Rear seat passengers also have side impact pelvic bags, and both rows are protected with side curtain bags that deploy in side crashes and rollovers. In the event the air bags are deployed, a system called EARS (Enhanced Accident Response System) automatically turns on the cabin lights and unlocks the doors to enable first responders to see and get into the vehicle. The system also shuts off the flow of fuel to the engine.

The long list of standard safety and security features on the base model also includes stability and traction control, tire pressure monitoring, electronic roll mitigation, brake assist that increases braking forces when an imminent collision is detected, hill-start assist, and the LATCH (Lower

Above: The Challenger remains as stylish as ever.

Below: Even in the 1950s, padded dashboards were becoming a major selling point as buyers became increasingly aware of the value of automotive safety.

INSTRUMENT PANEL SAFETY CUSHION OFFERS HEAD AND CHEST PROTECTION

The instrument panel safety cushion reduces the likelihood of head and chest injury during panic stops and crash impacts by absorbing energy and spreading the load. These cushions, offered for all Chrysler models, are made of polyurethane, a material having five times the energy absorbing capacity of sponge rubber.

CHRYSLER CORPORATION - Automotive Safety Engineering

Anchors and Tethers for Children) anchoring system for aftermarket child restraints. Available safety and security features on the Dart include ParkView rear backup camera, ParkSense rear park assist, and Rear Cross Path Detection.

While it's important that all Dodge products fare well in crash testing like those from the IIHS or the federal government's new car assessment program (NCAP), Dodge continues to focus on practical applications of new technology. The goal is to implement those things that it is convinced will make a difference in the real world in a way that will be very usable by the consumers.

A prime example of this new technology introduced on the 2014 Durango includes an available forward-collision warning system with crash mitigation. In addition to warning the driver that a collision is imminent, it also assists with vehicle braking to lessen the effects of an impact. Also available on the Durango is a new adaptive cruise control feature, which uses the same radar braking technology to bring the vehicle to a full stop in stop-and-go traffic.

Continuous product improvement was something John and Horace Dodge deeply believed in, and that spirit lives on in all Dodge products.

The Grand Caravan remains a family favorite.

# CHAPTER 15

# VIPER STRIKES

It's January 1989, and the Detroit Auto Show, a few years short of 100 years old, has for the first time transformed itself into the North American International Auto Show. The makeover is designed to underscore the global nature of the auto industry and to showcase the new luxury brands from Toyota and Nissan under their respective Lexus and Infiniti banners.

But the undeniable star of the first NAIAS is the Dodge Viper concept. The Viper was first championed by Lee Iacocca and developed under the watch of Chrysler President Bob Lutz, Engineering Vice President Francois Castaing, and Design Vice President Tom Gale. But they drew inspiration from an American automotive legend—Carroll Shelby.

An American supercar was desired, and Dodge was going to develop it. The open top 2-seater promised 400 horsepower from a monster 8.0-liter V-10 engine. A Spartan interior and side pipes recall Shelby's original Cobra. The Viper sent shockwaves through the enthusiast community,

The Viper concept, which promised 400 horsepower from an 8.0-liter V-10 engine, was the star of the 1989 North American International Auto Show. It also ushered in the process of vehicle development at Chrysler.

The Dodge Stratus incorporated the Intrepid's cab-forward design philosophy on a mid-size chassis. From this angle, the short front and rear overhangs are apparent.

neatly upstaging Chevrolet's launch of the production Corvette ZR-1 that following March in Geneva, a car that mustered just 375 horsepower.

At first blush, it appeared Dodge did the Viper just because it could—the corporation was flush with cash, and it could rely on the engineering expertise of recently acquired Lamborghini to help with the V-10 engine. More importantly, Dodge lacked a halo car like the Chevrolet Corvette or Ford Mustang in its lineup.

But the good times were about to come to a screeching halt, and a sales downturn saw Chrysler lose $1 billion in 1991 alone. Such a reversal meant some serious belt-tightening, and surely something as frivolous as a 400 horsepower 2-seat roadster would be one of the first things to go.

But the Viper survived to make it into production. That's because there was something else going on—something had happened within Dodge. The Viper's importance was more about how it was developed rather than what it was.

## A TEAM-BASED APPROACH TO SUCCESS

While Dodge had been successful in the 1980s on seemingly endless variants of the K-Car platform, the 1990s proved even more challenging. Dodge competed head-to-head with intense competition from all corners of the world offering sexy new imports that were refreshed on four-year cycles or less. Speed and agility were prized more than economies of scale and long spans between redesigns.

Castaing, who had joined Chrysler in the AMC acquisition, recognized these changes. Coming from an organization that had few resources in both cash and manpower, he saw the value in breaking down the silos that had developed in large manufacturers in which design would hand a car off to engineering, which would in turn hand the car off to manufacturing. It was a slow and cumbersome process that made it difficult to solve problems or make adjustments on the fly.

The Neon's fresh styling and affordable price enabled it to compete on equal footing with the best imported small cars of the 1990s.

Above: The 1993 Dodge Intrepid maximized cabin space and offered full-size comfort in a package that was closer to most mid-size cars of the day.

Above: In profile, the cab-forward design philosophy can be seen. The windshield's touchdown point is over the front wheels.

Below: The Dodge Caravan's styling continued to evolve, but not too radically, because its loyal customer base had conservative tastes. That didn't stop technical innovations like all-wheel drive on this '93 model.

Above: One of the so-called "cloud cars," the Dodge Stratus shared its platform with the Chrysler Cirrus and the Plymouth Breeze.

Castaing's solution was to create vehicle platform teams formed of members from design, engineering, manufacturing, marketing, and sales departments, all working in unison.

The team approach worked on the limited-edition Viper, which made it into production in three years at a time when most new products designed from the ground up took four or more. Dodge launched the Viper in 1992 with a limited run of 285, ramping up production at its small Mack Avenue assembly plant in Detroit to a high point of 3,083 in 1994.

Even before its launch, Viper turned heads when a prototype paced the 1991 Indianapolis 500 in May prior to the car's production that December. The official pace car was supposed to be the Dodge Stealth, a V-6-engined all-wheel-drive sport coupe shared with Mitsubishi that Dodge was rolling out that year. But the Viper was brought in to quell protests by the United Auto Workers.

Although Lutz celebrated the Viper's "Yestertech" bare-bones approach that dispensed with such modern features as anti-lock brakes and stability control, the car continued to be improved and refined over the years. The early models lacked exterior door handles and used fixed side curtains instead of traditional windows, and had a temporary top, known as the "toupee." The top was as difficult to assemble as a pup tent and could only be used if the car were driven at reduced speeds.

In 1996, Dodge launched the Viper GTS, a coupe version of the roadster. The GTS had conventional door glass and external door handles, features that would be added to the roadster when it returned to the lineup in 1997 as the RT/10 model. Again, the Viper saw duty as the Indy 500 pace car, this time with Lutz at the wheel for the 1996 race. He also had another reason for building the coupe—to race at Le Mans. The Viper GTS-R would go on to win the GT class in the French 24-hour race three years running, 1998–2000.

The Viper not only proved itself as an effective halo car for the Dodge organization, the cross-functional platform teams were having a profound effect on a new full-size family car called the Dodge Intrepid. This LH platform featured groundbreaking style, redefining the family car much the same way as the stylish Ford Taurus had done in 1986.

The Intrepid was unusual in two aspects. First, contrary to conventional practice in front-drive vehicles, the engine was mounted longitudinally instead of transversely, which had the advantage of allowing for a lower hood line and tighter turning circle. It also provided the option of building the car as either front-, rear-, or all-wheel drive, although the Intrepid was offered front-drive only throughout its lifespan. Second, the design was not only aerodynamic, but also the first of what would become known as "cab forward" designs from Design Chief Tom Gale. This approach had the touchdown point of the windshield nearly over the front wheels. By doing so, the shape maximized the cabin space and reduced the amount of front and rear overhang. Not only were the cars sleek, they had a tremendous amount of usable interior space.

Introduced in 1993, the Intrepid rode on a mid-size car wheelbase of 113 inches but offered a full-size car's cabin with seating for up to six with front and rear bench seats. Buyers could opt for a choice of two V-6 engines: the entry level 3.3-liter with 153 horsepower, or the step up to the 3.5-liter engine, which was rated at 214 horsepower.

The success of the LH cars quickly returned the company's health, and the profits in turn channeled back into major project initiatives, one of which was the Dodge Neon. This spiritual successor to the entry-level Omni and Shadow had an ambitious brief—it would prove once and for all that a small car could be built profitably in the United States.

Below: The Intrepid received its first major overhaul in 1998. This 2000 ES shows how large the cabin is to the relative length of the vehicle. Note the cross-hair grille design, adapted from the Ram and Viper.

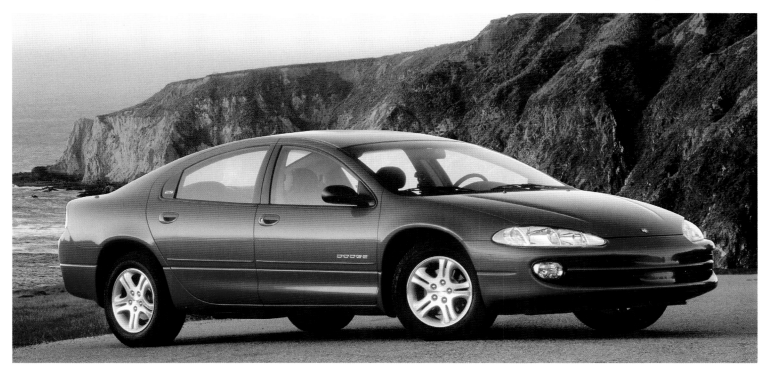

# SAY HELLO TO NEON

Dodge had one car in mind to succeed the entry-level Omni as the turn-of-the-century profitable compact: the Neon.

Because of high labor costs, conventional wisdom held that automakers built their entry-level subcompacts at a loss but needed to keep the factories running because of labor contracts (and also to meet federal fuel economy standards). Iacocca started Project Liberty to prove that conventional wisdom wrong.

The new PL platform rode on a 104-inch wheelbase and was powered by a 2.4-liter 4-cylinder engine in two states of tune: 132 or 150 horsepower. Both Dodge and Plymouth marketed the car as the Neon, and the only difference was the color of the badges—red for Dodge, and blue for Plymouth. Taking its cue from the 1991 concept car of the same name, the Neon had round headlamps that gave it a cute face at a time when most cars in the subcompact class sported rectangular headlamps. The Neon advertisements capitalized on this playful look with a campaign that simply said, "Hi."

The Neon, which was offered in both 2- and 4-door versions, was popular not only with the buying public but also among amateur racers. A special American Club Racer (ACR) package was

developed, along with a factory sponsored Neon Challenge racing series. The Neon would go on to win championships in the Sports Car Club of America's Showroom Stock C class.

The cab-forward design trend continued with the Dodge Stratus, a mid-market entry designed to compete with imports like the Honda Accord and Toyota Camry. Based on the JA platform, the Stratus offered a roomy cabin on a taut 108-inch wheelbase. Buyers could opt for either 4- or 6-cylinder engine power.

As these new cars were being phased in, the Dodge Shadow and Dodge Spirit—the last of the K-based dynasty—were being phased out by 1995. The Daytona, after undergoing a series of refreshes, was replaced by a new sport coupe called the Avenger, which was introduced in 1995 and built by Mitsubishi at its plant in Bloomington, Illinois.

Much less aggressive than the Daytona, the Avenger was more of a sporty coupe that shared its underpinnings with the Mitsubishi Galant. That car was sold through the 2000 model year.

Sales recovered in the mid-1990s, from a low point of 271,689 in 1992 to 425,109 in 1996. But the roller coaster ride was far from over. Sales would wax and wane with the economy and product offerings.

When the Dodge Neon was introduced in 1994, part of its mission was to show that a small car could be profitably built in the United States.

Right: In 1990, the V-6 engine carried over from 1989, as well as several safety and convenience features and upgrades.

Below: A major redesign of the Grand Caravan came in 1996. The vehicle was given smooth lines, rounded surfaces, and, for the first time ever, a driver's-side sliding door.

# THE RETURN OF RAM

Design played an important role not only in the car lineup, but also in trucks and minivans. While the minivans had a major facelift for the 1991 model year (including an all-wheel-drive option for the first time), the Caravan and Grand Caravan were totally redesigned in 1996. Based on an all-new platform designed to be a minivan from the ground up, this third-generation model featured a driver's side sliding door for the first time. Both the short-wheelbase Caravan and the long-wheelbase Grand Caravan had a smoother, more aerodynamic look but without sacrificing the utility of the traditional minivan package. Dodge understood its customers well enough to know that it didn't need to re-invent the minivan.

The 1990s resurgence in Dodge also saw a return of the Ram as a divisional mascot used on badging across the lineup. Another Dodge signature of this era was the recurring cross-hair grille theme that appeared on everything from the Neon up through the Ram truck.

This decade was a time of success, transitioning away from the K-Car, remaking the entire product lineup in just four short years (in 1996, the oldest car in the lineup was the Viper). It was also a time of a change in leadership. Lee Iacocca retired as Chrysler chairman and CEO in 1993, replaced by his handpicked successor, Robert Eaton, who was recruited from General Motors.

But Iacocca had second thoughts about turning over the reins of the company he left, and in 1996 he tried to get back into Chrysler via a hostile takeover bid by investor Kirk Kerkorian. That effort failed, but it opened the door to another period of new ownership, some product hits and misses, and ultimately, a financial crisis that would shake the very foundation of the marque created by John and Horace Dodge nearly a century earlier.

Below: The 1994 Dodge Ram.

# CHAPTER 16

# DODGE R/T

Like the Charger in the 1960s, the street Challenger of today is quite a bit different than the racer driven by Roger Penske in the NASCAR Nationwide series.

Dodge was not born in the crucible of motorsports. Although racing has been a part of the auto industry since its infancy, John and Horace Dodge were not participants. They were machinists who believed in making things—there are no records of Dodge being involved in the various races, time trials, or endurance events of old.

Proof of Dodge's value came from owning one. There was no race-on-Sunday, sell-on-Monday mindset. Even after the death of its founders, Dodge Brothers stayed away from motorsports, relying instead on touting the durability of its cars and trucks based on their use by the military and in the expeditions of archeologist Roy Chapman Andrews. Dodge vehicles were involved in five of his expeditions to Mongolia and Central China, including the Gobi Desert, between 1922 and 1928.

Walter P. Chrysler, on the other hand, believed in racing, sending Chryslers to the 24 Hours of Le Mans in 1925, 1928, 1929, and 1931. Chrysler-powered cars competed at the Indy 500, and both Chrysler and Imperial models paced the race. But for Dodge, there was virtually no motorsports program. During the first stock car race in 1936 at Daytona Beach, however, a Dodge was driven on the 3.2-mile course that included a paved section of Highway A1A and the beach. Midget racing car champ Bill Schindler privately entered a Dodge, finishing 18th out of 27 cars.

## GENTLEMEN, START YOUR ENGINES

It wasn't until Dodge introduced the Red Ram HEMI V-8 engine in 1953 that the division became a factor in racing. In that first year, Lee Petty won a NASCAR Grand National race in Palm Springs, Florida, the first for Dodge. On the west coast, Danny Eames hit 102.62 miles per hour in time trials on El Mirage Dry Lake in California, and then set 196 AAA stock car speed records at the Bonneville Salt Flats. And to round out the Red Ram's introduction, a Coronet equipped with the engine won that year's Mobilgas Economy Run. The following year, Dodge paced the Indianapolis 500 for the first time with a Royal 500 convertible.

Eames entered the Carrera Panamericana Mexican Road race in 1954 with a team of Dodge vehicles that swept the top three spots in the light stock category. According to the June 2011 issue of *Rod & Custom*, Eames returned to Bonneville in 1956 with four other drivers (including 1952 Indy 500 winner Troy Ruttman), driving a Dodge around a 10-mile circle for eight days. He covered 30,000 miles at an average speed of 150 miles per hour.

A Dodge Charger won the 1972 NASCAR championship.

Above: At the Bonneville Salt Flats, a team of drivers ran a 1956 Dodge over 30,000 miles in eight days.

Below: A latecomer to motorsports, Dodge began slowly by participating in the Mobil fuel-economy run and by setting various speed and endurance records.

Left: Originally developed in 1963 as a racing engine, this Ramcharger V-8 engine was upsized from 413 to 426 cubic inches. Note the dual 4-barrel carburetors.

Below, right: The modified Coronet was used for drag racing. Not only was its wheelbase shortened from 115 to 110 inches, but the front and rear axles were repositioned 10 and 15 inches forward respectively to improve the car's weight distribution.

Dodge was also present in NASCAR's new convertible division in 1956, with Marvin Panch earning a sole victory that year. In Grand National, Lee Petty ran a Coronet 2-door sedan with the D-500 engine optioning and won two races, finishing fourth overall in the standings.

In 1957, however, the Automobile Manufacturers Association announced a ban on advertising race wins as well as direct factory support to teams. Although the factories agreed to this self-imposed ban, many of the speed parts they had developed in their racing program were offered in special fleet and police "packages" that more often than not found their way into the hands of racers. Still, despite some of this back door support, Dodge did not play a major role in stock car racing for nearly five years.

Drag racing, however, was another story. These efforts began modestly with a group of drag racing Chrysler engineers who tinkered with a new V-8 engine on their own time. The new V-8 engines featured wedge-shaped combustion chambers and were introduced for the 1958 model year.

Part of that development included using a so-called "long horn" induction system, which they dubbed a ram's horn and finally called it ram induction. And that was the inspiration for this informal group to start calling themselves the Ramchargers. While their first car, the High and Mighty, was actually a 1949 Plymouth, they eventually settled on using Dodge vehicles, and won their first national title in 1961. Out of their work came Max Wedge V-8 engines that dominated drag racing throughout the 1960s. First introduced in 1962, the Max Wedge displaced 413 cubic inches and made 410 horsepower. A year later it was bumped up to the 426 and offered in a 1963 competition-only package making 425 horsepower.

The group's hobby had become an important technical and promotional tool for Dodge. Not only did their engineering make it into production as competition options, the Ramchargers also campaigned two factory-backed cars dubbed *Candymatics* for their candy apple red stripes and

SHORT-WHEELBASE, LIGHT-WEIGHT DODGE DRAG RACER

This 1965 Dodge Coronet will be out for AFX and ultra stock drag racing crowns. The 115-inch wheelbase has been shortened to 110 by moving the rear wheels forward 15 inches and front wheels ahead 10 inches providing improved weight distribution. Rear quarter-panel appearance is accomplished by fusing two panels together. Fiberglas parts, available through Plaza Fibreglas Mfg., 24 West Lane Ct., Dearborn, Mich., include hood and scoop, front bumper, front fenders and doors, instrument panel and deck lid. Parts total 80 lbs. Special steel "K" member, weighing 18 lbs., results in 25 lb. front weight savings. Another 25 lbs. are saved with use of Dodge Dart front spindles, brakes and brake drums.

From: Shively Motors, 801 Lincoln Way West, Chambersburg, Pa.     (65-185)

Top: The stock street 1969 Charger was a far cry from its winged racing cousin.

Inset: Built specifically for winning at NASCAR, the Charger Daytona included a high rear wing, flush rear window, and unique front nose for aerodynamic improvement.

automatic transmissions. The factory-backed Ramchargers raced throughout the 1960s and early '70s before disbanding in 1974. The outfit did spawn an aftermarket speedshop and parts business that survives to this day.

Other significant drag racing teams of the era also included Roger Lindamood and his Color Me Gone Dodge Coronet, "Big Daddy" Don Garlits, "Wild Bill" Shrewsberry and his wheelstanding L.A. Dart. And then there was Bill "Maverick" Golden, who campaigned Dodge super stocks and later drove the factory-backed Little Red Wagon, a wheelstanding Dodge pickup.

Meanwhile, the AMA ban began to unravel when Henry Ford II said his company would no longer support it. Ford began full factory programs in stock cars, and more importantly, in Le Mans.

Chrysler president Lynn Townsend, looking to tap into the youth market, shortly thereafter announced that Chrysler was back in racing.

To counter Ford's dominance in NASCAR, Chrysler built a new 426-cubic-inch HEMI engine for the 1964 season. Although Plymouth was carrying the banner for the corporation—Richard Petty won the Daytona 500 that year—Dodge cars equipped with the same engine performed well, with Jim Pascal taking fifth in the race in a car owned by legendary racer Cotton Owens.

So overpowering were the HEMI engines that NASCAR banned their use in 1965, and Chrysler boycotted the series. When Chrysler announced that it would be building a "street HEMI" engine for regular production cars, the engine was readmitted for the 1966 season, just in time to be used in the all-new Dodge Charger. It became the car to beat, winning 18 races and propelling David Pearson to his first Grand National title in a Cotton Owens car. But the Charger's dominance was short-lived—the following season was all Richard Petty in a Plymouth. Petty won 27 races, including ten straight wins to collect his second championship in just four years.

# BREAKING THE 200 MILE PER HOUR BARRIER

The 1968 redesign of the Charger, while pleasing to the eye, had some serious aerodynamic issues. Both the inset front grille and flying buttress C-pillars added a tremendous amount of lift and made it difficult for the car to run competitively. A hurried redesign that eliminated the buttresses and grafted a new flush grille on the limited run Charger 500 enabled the cars to win 22 races in 1969.

But in looking to get that competitive edge back, Dodge created one of the wildest race cars that could be bought for street use: Charger Daytona. Quickly approved by Dodge Vice President and General Manager Robert "Bob" McCurry, the Daytona featured a high rear wing, flush rear window, and a sharp nose that incorporated hideaway headlamps.

The Daytona became the first to break the 200-mile-per-hour barrier on a closed course when Buddy Baker set the record on March 24, 1970, during a test at Talledega. Bobby Isaac won the championship that year in the K&K Insurance Dodge Daytona, and a year later, Isaac made it to the Bonneville Salt Flats where he broke 28 speed records, including a run of over 217 miles per hour.

Looking to get speeds back under control, NASCAR mandated smaller 305-cubic-inch engines for 1971, and soon the winged cars were gone. Richard Petty ran both Plymouth and Dodge and won his fourth Grand National title in 1972, switching back to Dodge Chargers during the next season. He went on to win the championship two more times by 1975.

One of Dodge's best years in NASCAR occurred in 1974. The division won 10 races and the manufacturer's title. But by the late 1970s, the factory NASCAR effort wound down, and the last win by a Dodge in Winston Cup came November 20, 1977, at Ontario with Neil Bonnet behind the wheel. The era closed in 1985, when Phil Good drove a Dodge at Pocono to a 30th place finish.

Throughout the 1970s and early 1980s, factory racing became secondary in importance as Dodge and Chrysler struggled through tough economic times. Just as the glory days of the muscle car era had passed, so had Dodge's interest in direct involvement in motorsports. It would take a new generation of performance cars to rekindle that spirit.

Richard Petty campaigned a Dodge Charger in NASCAR in 1972.

Although Dodge left NASCAR at the end of the 2012 season, performance continued with the introduction of the 2012 Charger Super Bee.

This is a Dodge Viper SRT coupe; its predecessors raced across Europe to victory at the 24 Hours of Le Mans race.

## THE ROAD TO LE MANS

In the mid-1980s, Carroll Shelby's program of building hot versions of the front-drive Charger opened that door. Team Shelby, racing in the SCCA Escort Endurance Series, won three of the six races on the schedule, including two 24-hour races in a Shelby Charger.

Dodge also became involved in the International Race of Champion (IROC), providing identically prepared Daytonas (rear-drive racing versions of the front-drive street cars) from 1990 to 1993, and again in 1994 and 1995 under the Avenger.

While the Dodge Neon was introduced in 1994 as an affordable, U.S.-built compact, the coupe version proved to be the hot ticket in amateur racing. Dodge understood the car's appeal and made it even more competitive by offering the American Club Racer (ACR) package that featured a tuned suspension and minimal options to keep weight down. The Neon ACR counts three consecutive SCCA Showroom Stock C class titles in the mid-1990s among its 20 national titles in road racing and solo events.

The introduction of the Dodge Viper in 1992 took Dodge's motorsports ambitions to the international stage. In 1996, when the second-generation Viper debuted as the GTS coupe, an R or racing version was also unveiled to announce a plan to take the 2-seat sports car to Le Mans.

Under the direction of France's Oreca team, the Viper GTS-R (badged as Chrysler in Europe)

won its first international sports car race at Hockenheim in 1997, and then went on to take the GT class at the 24 Hours of Le Mans in 1998, 1999, and 2000, as well as becoming the first production-based American car to take an overall win at the 24 Hours of Daytona. Adding to its impressive victory list, the Viper also prevailed in 24-hour races at Spa and the Nurburgring, winning the former in 2001–2002 and the latter in 1999, 2001, and 2002.

Meanwhile, Dodge's long road back to NASCAR started in 1996 with the Ram truck in the Craftsman Truck series. The division won two manufacturer titles and a total of 46 of 99 races between 2001–2004 before bowing out of the program in 2009.

On the car side, Dodge returned to NASCAR in 2001 with the Intrepid R/T and no fewer than five teams. Differing from the V-6–engined front-drive production model, the rear-drive Cup cars were powered by V-8 engines but carried graphics to suggest the street car. The Intrepid was replaced for one season (2007) by the Avenger, and in 2008, the Avenger was in turn replaced by the Charger, a vehicle much closer to the racecar in that it offered V-8 engine and rear-drive in production trim. Eventually, only one team (Penske) was campaigning Dodge by 2012. Although it announced that it would run Ford in 2013—effectively ending Dodge's NASCAR involvement—Penske delivered the driver's championship with Brad Keselowski, allowing the Dodge brand to go out on a high note.

# DRAG CITY

To this day, however, Dodge continues be in the top tier of drag racing with representation in Top Fuel, Funny Car, and Pro Stock classes.

In 2009, Mopar, Chrysler's aftermarket and speed parts division, offered 100 factory-built Dodge Challengers in its Drag Pak program, which was designed to commemorate the 40th Anniversary of a similar program that offered Dodge Dart vehicles with HEMI engines to drag racers. The cars, powered by a 6.1-liter HEMI engine, were lightened by 1,000 pounds and equipped with polycarbonate windows, Viper-style front seats, and a composite lift-off hood with a functional air scoop. Although the original Dart cars equipped with HEMI engines were regular production with VINs, the Challenger Drag Pak cars have no VINs and are not street legal. In 2011, the program offered the 8.4-liter V-10 engine from the Viper.

Meanwhile, the formation of the Ram brand in 2009 and the SRT brand in 2012 to market full-size trucks and high-performance cars, respectively, may spell the end to large factory racing programs at Dodge. While Dodge may no longer be in NASCAR, Dodge remains strongly linked with motorsports and performance cars, including top fuel, funny car, and pro stock. Plus, with the Dart, the spiritual successor to the Neon in SCCA club racing, the motorsports torch will be passed on.

And in a way, Dodge's racing heritage has come full circle, returning to the drag strips and local tracks by offering products that are fun to drive, affordable, and durable. As racers know all too well, to finish first, you must first finish. Dodge's reputation for dependability will certainly keep this brand in the hunt.

Dodge enjoys a rich history of racing. Below, a 2014 Challenger shows off the Mopar Drag Package.

# CHAPTER 17

# MERGING INTERESTS

As the new millennium approached, Chrysler management, spooked by the Kirk Kerkorian hostile takeover attempt and an uncertain market, began looking for a partner that would not only offer greater cost efficiencies and scale, but could also help expand the global reach of all its brands.

It was a period of consolidation in the auto industry, and automakers the world over were either merging or forming joint ventures to compensate for one weakness or another. The 1999 Renault and Nissan deal was one example—Nissan was strong in Asia and the United States, while Renault's best markets were in Europe. Meanwhile, Volkswagen Group went on a buying spree, gobbling up Bentley and Lamborghini, the latter having passed from Chrysler to private owners after Iacocca's retirement.

The Dodge Dart GT, Challenger R/T, and Charger R/T, each outfitted with the performance-boosting Scat Pack factory stage kit.

Above: For 2003 the Viper received a major makeover for the first time since 1996, which included bumping the displacement of the V-10 engine up to 8.3 liters.

Right: The 2006 Dodge Challenger concept paved the way for a modern incarnation of the 1970 classic.

Bottom: The Challenger rides on a shortened LX platform used for the Charger and Magnum.

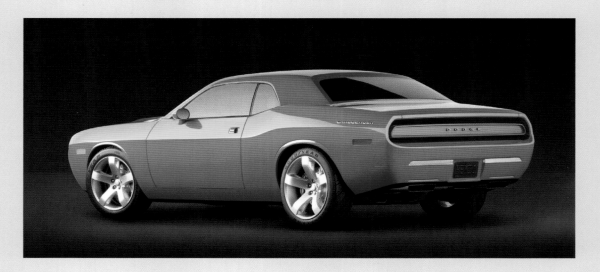

Chrysler had thought it had found a good fit in Daimler-Benz, the German parent of Mercedes-Benz. The so-called "merger of equals" would complement each other—Mercedes would cover the luxury and European markets, while Chrysler would continue to serve the mass market..

Soon after Chrysler CEO Bob Eaton and Daimler Chief Jürgen Schrempp announced the merger in 1998, it became apparent that it wasn't so equal. Bob Lutz soon left the company, and Eaton also retired. In 1999, Jim Holden was named President of Chrysler. Dieter Zetsche, who came over from Mercedes-Benz car operations, replaced Holden in 2000.

Despite all these changes at the top of the organization, the Dodge product blitz that had started in the 1990s was by no means exhausted. The second-generation Intrepid debuted, and its styling took the cab-forward design approach to the next level. Introduced in 1998, the Intrepid sported smooth flowing lines and a longer and wider body on the same 113.0-inch wheelbase. It offered upgraded interiors and new powertrain choices, including a 200-horsepower 2.7-liter V-6 engine or a 225-horsepower 3.2-liter V-6 engine. Both were smaller in displacement yet more powerful than the 3.3- and 3.5-liter engines they replaced.

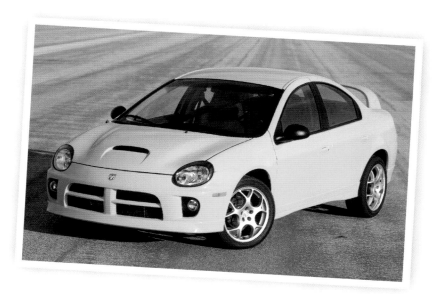

The Dodge SRT-4 was launched in 2003 with a 215-horsepower, 2.4-liter turbocharged engine, quickly enhanced to 230 horsepower for 2004 and available with up to 300 horsepower with the Mopar Stage III kit.

For the 2000 model year, the Neon was all new, with a more upscale treatment and a standard 132-horsepower, 2.0-liter, 4-cylinder engine or a 150-horsepower 2.0-liter in the R/T. Building on the sport-compact craze and the 2000 concept vehicle, the SRT-4 was launched in the 2003 model year with a 2.4-liter, turbocharged and intercooled, 215-horsepower, 4-cylinder engine, resulting in a 0–60-mile-per-hour time of 5.8 seconds. For 2004, it was bumped up to 230 horsepower and continued its very enthusiastic following.

The Stratus was all new for 2001, in either sedan or coupe form, with an available 2.7- liter, 200-horsepower V-6 engine. Also in 2001, the Caravan and Grand Caravan received a major makeover in 2001—the styling continued to evolve, becoming more refined without going to the extremes that would alienate its conservative audience. While minivan buyers appreciated the clean good looks of their family vehicles, they were much more interested in how they functioned. Dodge responded to those desires by offering power sliding side doors, a power rear lift gate, and more powerful 3.3- and 3.8-liter V-6 engines. Two years later, to the relief of long-suffering parents, a factory-installed rear-seat entertainment system was offered for the first time.

In 2003, the Viper received its first major overhaul since the 1996 refresh that introduced the coupe. This all-new model, introduced first as the RT/10 roadster and then followed by the GTS coupe, featured a bump in engine displacement from 8.0 to 8.3 liters, and a corresponding increase in output to an even 500 horsepower.

During this period, Tom Gale's designers were not only busy with the constant flow of production launches—they also produced a stunning array of concept cars for the auto show circuit. While some were readily apparent previews of upcoming production models, there was also a steady parade of vehicles that not only explored future design themes, but also toyed with segments in which Dodge conceivably could compete—if there was enough money to fund the program.

Right: Among the concepts shown during the 1990s, few were more exciting than the Dodge Demon, a tidy 2-door sports car.

The HEMI engine returned to the Dodge car lineup beneath the hood of the Dodge Magnum in 2005. The 5.7-liter V-8 engine had many advanced technical features, including multiple displacement, which allowed it to cruise in 4-cylinder mode.

# RESURRECTING REAR DRIVE

One of the greatest legacies to emerge from the DaimlerChrysler experience was the return of rear-wheel drive to the passenger car portfolio. Dodge did have rear-drive products in the form of the Viper and the trucks, but since the Diplomat had been discontinued in 1985, all of Dodge's mainstream passenger cars were front-drive.

For the 2005 model year, Dodge replaced the LH platform Intrepid with a new rear-drive architecture called LX. And instead of having a 4-door sedan at the top of its passenger car line, Dodge proffered up the Magnum wagon in both rear- and all-wheel drive. The Magnum featured a wide range of engines, including a 190-horsepower 2.7-liter V-6 engine, a 250-horsepower 3.5-liter V-6 engine, and the powerful 340-horsepower 5.7-liter HEMI V-8 engine.

The Magnum was bold. It had a blunt nose with a large square grille sporting the cross-hair grille theme of the Ram pickup. Riding on a 120-inch wheelbase, Magnum's wagon configuration was a controversial choice at a time when 3-box sedans were the body style of choice in the family car market. But this strategy was meant to clearly differentiate the Dodge offering in this segment from the more traditional Chrysler 300 sedan, which shared the same mechanicals. While Magnum sales topped 50,000 in 2005, Dodge dropped the car after 2008, even though it had introduced a minor facelift for that final model year.

Dealers who wanted a more traditional 4-door sedan were given the Charger for the 2006 model year. That car not only proved to be popular with consumers, but it was well accepted in the fleet market, especially law enforcement, which liked the Charger for its rear-drive layout. The Charger's engine specifications and options were similar to those on the Magnum.

Left: A year after the wagon-based Magnum was introduced, Dodge brought out a sedan that resurrected the Charger nameplate.

Left: Replacing the mid-size Stratus sedan in the line, the Avenger's shape mimics the look of the full-size Charger.

Below: The Dodge Magnum, offered in rear- and all-wheel-drive versions, stirred up a bit of controversy with its station-wagon styling, but it remains to this day one of the most unique offerings from Dodge and has a very passionate owner base.

In its final year, the 2008 Magnum offered refreshed styling and up to 425 horsepower from a 6.1-liter HEMI V-8 engine.

Both the Magnum and Charger were also offered in high-performance SRT guises that included the use of a 6.1-liter HEMI V-8 engine producing 425 horsepower.

Just as the Magnum wagon replaced the Intrepid sedan at the top of the line, on the entry-level side of the ledger, the Neon was replaced by the Caliber for the 2007 model year. This tall 4-door hatch was kind of a cross between a small SUV and a traditional station wagon. The hope was to cash in on the emerging crossover segment in which vehicles sported the rugged looks of a traditional SUV but were in fact modeled on car-based front-drive platforms, which were lighter and more fuel-efficient than traditional truck-based vehicles.

The Caliber's husky design showcased the bold Ram pickup-inspired face and its signature crosshair grille design. The platform used was based on a modified design developed with Mitsubishi. The Caliber offered a 1.8-liter 4-cylinder engine making 148 horsepower, while a 2.0-liter engine making 158 horsepower was optional. A 2.4-liter, 173-horsepower engine was also offered in the R/T. The base engine was mated to a 5-speed manual transmission, while the larger engine used a continuously variable automatic transaxle. Caliber's interior was extremely functional and contained many innovative features like the millennial targeted sound bar option, located in the rear hatch, providing musical entertainment for impromptu parking lot parties. An SRT-4 version of the Caliber was also offered, and included a stout 285 horsepower 2.4-liter turbo engine.

Left: The Caliber's front end carried strong styling cues taken from the successful Ram pickup. The large crosshair grille was a theme used across the entire Dodge lineup.

Below: Building off the tremendous success of the Neon-derived SRT-4, the Caliber SRT-4 was introduced in 2008 with a 285-horsepower intercooled turbo engine.

Above: The modern Challenger recalls its classic muscle-car roots.

Dodge also wanted to capitalize on the trend of buyers shifting from cars to trucks, so Dodge introduced the Nitro, a compact SUV that shared mechanicals with the Jeep Liberty. This upright 4-door featured V-6 engine power and choice of rear- or all-wheel drive. With a four-year production run totaling just 175,000 vehicles, the Nitro was discontinued after the 2011 calendar year.

Meanwhile, in the middle of the lineup, Dodge replaced its Stratus mid-size sedan with the Avenger. This 4-door front-drive sedan had styling similar to the larger Charger in that it incorporated a large cross-hair grille, slab sides, and upswept rear fenders. In 2010, the Avenger received extensive interior, exterior, and powertrain upgrades, including the adoption of the 283-horsepower Pentastar V-6 engine, making it a hit with consumers and quickly becoming one of the best-selling Dodge vehicles in 2012 and 2013. Not only was the styling less fluid than the sleek Stratus and more in-your-face with the large grille, the interior also suffered from the same cost-cutting measures that afflicted the Caliber. Still, Dodge stuck with the car, upgrading its interior to see sales strengthen on the basis of a 2011 refresh.

At the 2006 North American International Auto Show, Dodge stole the show with the introduction of the Challenger concept, a re-creation of the first-generation car. This time the Challenger sat on a shortened 116.0-inch wheelbase from the LX platform that underpinned the Charger sedan.

With its clean lines and muscular proportions, the Challenger entered limited production by 2008. Only 6,400 models were produced for the U.S., and they were all SRT8 models equipped with 425-horsepower 6.1-liter HEMI V-8 engines. When regular production commenced for the 2009 model year, the Challenger was offered with three powertrain choices: the 253-horsepower 3.5-liter V-6 engine; the 375-horspower 5.7-liter HEMI V-8 engine; and the SRT8 model with the 425-horsepower 6.1-liter HEMI V-8 engine.

The Dodge Grand Caravan was redesigned in 2001 and shared the bold crosshair grille theme that became a signature of the division.

With the introduction of the 5.7-liter HEMI V-8 engine in the Ram pickup, it wasn't long before the engine returned to the car lineup in the Dodge Magnum, which was launched in 2005.

## GOVERNMENTAL OVERSIGHT

The first decade of the new century was filled with uncertainty. The 9/11 terrorist attacks that destroyed the World Trade Center in New York and damaged the Pentagon resulted in a downturn in the economy that affected all automakers. New product initiatives helped the industry claw back some, but the pressures to maintain sales momentum through costly incentives took a huge toll on the bottom line. Cash reserves were quickly depleted, and the pressure to cut costs adversely affected the product. With an increasingly bleak future, Daimler began seeking an exit strategy, seeking a buyer for Chrysler, which had booked 2006 losses of $1.5 billion. The merger of equals would last less than a decade.

It's often said that the more things change, the more they stay the same. No truer words could be spoken about Dodge. The company founded by two hard-working brothers found itself in the hands of a New York investment banking firm within several years of the brothers' deaths. In 2007, Wall Street again played a significant role in the company's history, as Daimler unloaded Chrysler to a venture capital firm by the name of Cerberus Capital Management.

Cerberus, named after the mythical three-headed dog—the hound of Hell guarding the gates to the netherworld—announced a high-minded goal of building Chrysler back up as an all-American auto manufacturer. In practice, the investment bank underestimated the capital requirements needed to successfully run the automaker. In addition, it brought in top management, including CEO Robert Nardelli, a former head of Home Depot who had no experience in the auto industry.

The ink had barely dried on the agreement when the real estate equities bubble burst, the stock market crashed, and Wall Street was rocked by the failure of Lehman Brothers. Car sales dropped from an annual rate of just over 17 million to approximately 10 million. Total Dodge sales fell from a peak of over 600,000 to around 325,000. Dodge was again threatened with extinction; while it had avoided a crisis before thanks to the government-backed loans in 1979, this time it appeared that there was no way out. It was time for yet another appeal to the government to save it.

# CHAPTER 18

# MY OTHER CAR IS AN SUV

Aside from the invention of the minivan—a game changer in its own right—the other phenomenon affecting the auto industry in the closing decades of the twentieth century was the shift to trucks, and more specifically, to sport/utility vehicles as a form of personal transportation.

    The impetus behind this trend can be found in the two-tiered nature of Corporate Average Fuel Economy standards (CAFE) that had separate, more lenient schedules for trucks. When the rules were written, trucks were employed primarily for commercial use—no one envisioned that they would become the family vehicle of choice once traditional V-8 engined full-size sedans and station wagons were downsized or eliminated altogether to meet the more stringent passenger car regulations.

This wagon version of the 1948 Power Wagon is the forerunner to the modern full-size SUV.

A PLACE IN THE SUN is offered for any user of Dodge Truck recreational vehicles. Campers go first class with many of the comforts of home. The three Sportsman wagon and van, camper conversions in foreground show variations of the 90 or 108-wheelbase models that sleep up to five. At upper left is one of the many Dodge pickup models with slide-on camper body fitted onto the truck bed. At top is the apartment-size Dodge Motor Home by Travco.

From Dodge Public Relations, P.O. Box 1259, Detroit, Michigan 48231   (68-2644)

Trucks have a long history of personal use. The first instances were primarily recreational vehicles. This photo depicts the wide range of choices from Dodge for 1968, from A-100 van campers up through a purpose-built RV.

Well before the oil crises of the 1970s and the implementation of CAFE, however, people-carrying, truck-based vehicles were part of the automotive landscape, albeit on a limited scale. These forerunners to the modern SUV trace their roots back to the World War II carryalls that were part of the WC truck line.

Unlike the Power Wagon and pickup, which were introduced right after the war, Dodge's carryall variant to compete with the Chevrolet Suburban wasn't introduced until 1954. The 2-wheel-drive version was called the Town Wagon, and a light delivery vehicle called the Town Panel, were built off the same chassis as the standard Dodge C-Series pickup truck. A 4x4 version was introduced in 1957 as a Power Wagon Town Wagon. These vehicles were manufactured until 1966, when the introduction of the new A-100 vans in both passenger and commercial trim eliminated the need for these people-moving and cargo-carrying pickup-based trucks.

Dodge returned to the full-size SUV market in 1974, this time with a 2-door Ramcharger, which was pitted against the Ford Bronco and Chevrolet Blazer. Like those vehicles, it was built off a full-size pickup truck and could be equipped with either 2- or 4-wheel drive. The Ramcharger remained a staple in the lineup through two generations until 1993 and even after, as the Mexican-built truck was adapted to the new Ram pickup and sold south of the border through 2001.

During the 1980s, the Dodge Caravan, like the A-100 before it, filled a need for a people mover in the lineup, and as a result, Dodge stayed away from developing a 4-door full-size SUV based on the Ramcharger to compete with the Chevy Suburban. However, with the introduction of the Jeep Cherokee in 1984, a new market for mid-size 4x4 SUVs developed. Buyers liked the higher seating position and practicality of four doors as well as the all-weather and go-anywhere capability of all-wheel drive.

The success of the Cherokee sparked a boom in both mid-size and large SUVs. Although Dodge was late to the market, it capitalized on the success of its mid-size Dakota by offering the Durango in 1998, an SUV that was sized to compete with the mid-size five-passenger Chevrolet

Dodge's first modern full-size SUV was the 1974 Ramcharger, which was built off the division's full-size pickup truck.

Left: Instead of building a full-size SUV, Dodge created the Durango, which was based on the mid-size Dakota pickup platform and neatly slotted between traditional mid- and full-size SUVs.

Below: The Ramcharger remained a mainstay in the Dodge lineup through the 1980s, although the division decided against making a 4-door version.

The Power Wagon concept vehicle.

The influence of the Power Wagon concept vehicle can be seen on this 2004 redesign of the Dodge Durango.

Trailblazer and Ford Explorer, but offered three-row seating for up to eight passengers like the much larger Chevy Suburban and Ford Expedition.

The first two generations of the Durango used body-on-frame construction much like the original Town Wagon. Riding on a 116.2-inch wheelbase, it was initially offered with a standard 175-horsepower 3.9-liter V-6 engine and two optional V-8 engines; a 5.2-liter engine making 230-horsepower; and a top spec 5.9-liter Magnum V-8 engine with 245 horses. Launched with 4-wheel drive only, the Durango came with a 4-speed automatic transmission. A rear-drive version was added to the lineup in its second year. By 2000, an all-new 4.7-liter V-8 engine making 235 horsepower replaced the 5.2-liter engine.

The design of the first generation Durango was similar to the Dakota in that it had the stepped fender look and large cross-hair grille treatment of the full-size Ram pickup. And even though it featured a truck chassis underneath, the Durango was outfitted with a level of creature comforts that made it a modern equivalent of the traditional full-size family station wagon of the '60s and '70s.

The all-new second-generation Durango introduced in 2004 grew larger and now rode on a 119.3-inch wheelbase and featured a larger cabin. It was officially classified as a full-size SUV, although its exterior dimensions were still tidier than the competition. The redesigned Durango's bolder grille, large headlamps, and muscular wheel arches were influenced heavily by the Dodge Power Box concept. The 4.7-liter V-8 engine was carried over, while a new 210-horsepower, 3.7-liter V-6 engine and 335-horsepower 5.7-liter HEMI V-8 engine debuted.

Three years later, Durango received a facelift that eliminated the stepped-fender look that had been a design cue since its introduction. Even though the growth in the SUV market was fostered by the two-tier approach to fuel economy standards, these vehicles were not immune to demands for better efficiency as gas prices rose. For the 2009 model year, Dodge introduced a hybrid version of the Durango that featured a new dual-mode electric hybrid system developed in conjunction with GM and BMW. This technology mated a 5.7-liter HEMI V-8 engine, which also featured displacement on demand that allowed the engine to operate in a 4-cylinder mode, to a transmission that incorporated electric drive in low speeds. This system also benefited from a stop-start feature that turned the engine off when the vehicle was at rest. As a result, the Durango offered a 25 percent increase in fuel economy—much of it a gain in the "in the city" rating—which jumped from about 13 miles per gallon to 20 miles per gallon.

## RISING TIDES

The financial crisis of 2008 and Chrysler's subsequent bankruptcy in 2009 interrupted Durango production. The Newark assembly plant was shut down, and production moved to the Jefferson North plant, which built a new Durango employing unit-body construction. Leveraging architecture developed for the successful Jeep Grand Cherokee, the 2011 Durango featured a 119.9-inch wheelbase and retained its three-row seating capability. The hybrid was dropped and the engines updated to include the 290-horsepower 3.6-liter Pentastar V-6 engine and the 360-horsepower 5.7-liter HEMI V-8 engine. The Durango underwent a refresh again for 2014 with new front and rear treatments, an upgraded interior, and the introduction of a new 8-speed automatic transmission replacing the previous 6- and 5-speed automatics.

While Dodge had the mid- to full-size SUV market covered with the Durango, the compact segment was growing rapidly, and a new model, the Nitro, was introduced in 2007 to address that market. Sharing the same architecture as the second-generation Jeep Liberty, the Nitro was slightly larger, riding on a longer 108.8-inch wheelbase. Although the Nitro was offered with a choice of rear- or all-wheel drive, it was aimed squarely at the on-road personal use market, while the Liberty, which had a 106.1-inch wheelbase, was targeted at those who wanted a more traditional off-roader.

The Nitro came with a choice of a 3.7- or 4.0-liter V-6 engine, with respective outputs of 210 and 255 horsepower. Transmissions included a 6-speed manual or a 4-speed automatic on the 3.7-liter V-6, and a 5-speed automatic with the 4.0-liter engine. Nitro was noted for its class-leading towing capacity of 5,000 lbs. with the larger engine.

The 4-door Nitro had seating for five passengers, and its styling was a straightforward roomy shape with a large grille featuring Dodge's crosshair design. Sales peaked immediately with nearly 75,000 sold in its first year, but then dropped in half the next and to about a third in subsequent model years.

The Dodge Durango was freshened for the 2014 model year, adding the signature Dodge-brand LED racetrack taillamps and a new eight-speed automatic transmission that delivers an improvement in fuel economy and enhances performance.

Above: The Durango shifted to the Jeep Grand Cherokee platform after going on hiatus for the 2010 model year. The Dodge is built alongside the Grand Cherokee at Chrysler's Jefferson East assembly plant in Detroit.

Below: Based on the Dodge Avenger mid-size car platform, the Journey is a new breed of crossover that provides a carlike ride with the looks and all-wheel-drive capability of an SUV.

Above: Adding to the flexibility of the Journey is its flat-folding seats, which create a huge cargo area.

The Nitro was born from a lengthened Jeep Liberty platform and differentiated itself with available 20-inch wheels.

Nitro's short-lived run also reflected a change in the SUV market, which was not only downsizing, but also morphing into a new class of vehicles called crossovers. Unlike the traditional SUV, which can trace its roots back to trucks with body-on-frame construction, longitudinal engines, and a bias towards rear-drive, these new vehicles share their platforms with front-drive cars equipped with transverse-mounted engines. The difference is that the crossover offers a carlike ride and amenities with optional all-wheel drive and a design inspired by traditional SUVs.

Dodge tried to tap into this emerging trend with the 4-cylinder powered Caliber in 2007, using a car-based platform and a hatchback body that looked like a small SUV. Offered in either front- or all-wheel-drive, the Caliber replaced the Neon sedan, but like the Nitro, it never found a large audience. Part of the problem is that the newer crossovers tended to be larger, more often than not had V-6 engine power, and featured a higher, command-of-the-road seating position.

A much more successful entry was the 2009 Journey. Based on the mid-size Avenger architecture, the Journey rides on a 113.8-inch wheelbase. This mid-size package offers the family-friendly roominess of a minivan or wagon. By offering a choice of either a 173-horsepower 2.4-liter 4-cylinder engine or 235-horsepower 3.5-liter V-6 engine, the Journey appeals to a much wider audience with a base five-passenger front-drive model starting around $20,000, up through a fully-loaded V-6 engine with all-wheel drive and seating for seven. In 2011, the vehicle was refreshed as the 3.5-liter V-6 engine was replaced by the more powerful 283-horsepower Pentastar 3.6-liter V-6 engine. Sales of the Journey have continued to climb since its introduction, growing to nearly 80,000 in 2012. A version of the Journey has been rebadged as the Fiat Freemont for sale in Europe.

With Durango and Journey, Dodge has two strong entries in a market that is continuing to grow. Both products have a bright future thanks to their efficient designs and the fact that they share architectures with other vehicles in the Chrysler portfolio. Despite these shared underpinnings, both models have design, packaging, and value pricing unique to the Dodge brand.

# CHAPTER 19

# RENAISSANCE

The Cerberus era was mercifully short—shorter even than the Dillon, Read experience at Dodge some 80 years earlier.

That's not to say that the change in ownership was not a wrenching experience. When the market crashed in 2008 (and car sales with it—Chrysler sales dropped 36 percent in one year), the administration of President George W. Bush approved emergency loans for both General Motors and Chrysler. Forget Iacocca's $1.5 billion—Chrysler received more than twice that number, some $4 billion in funding.

Instead of preventing bankruptcy proceedings, though, the funding only postponed them. In 2009, under President Barack Obama, an auto industry taskforce from the Treasury Department arranged structured Chapter 11 bankruptcy proceedings in April that eliminated most of the company's debt and provided access to much needed capital. Ownership of the new company

The touchstones for the essence of the Dodge brand are the Challenger (left) and Charger (right). These models are designated to carry the division's special 100th anniversary edition packages, which will be produced between January and July 2014.

Above: The Dodge Journey blends the people-moving 7-passenger capacity of a minivan with SUV-inspired styling. In addition to being sold in the United States. and abroad as a Dodge, one variant is also marketed as the Fiat Fremont in Italy.

Below: Across the line, Dodge stresses the four pillars of its brand: performance, technology, versatility, and value.

was transferred to a consortium that included the United Auto Worker's Voluntary Employ Benefit Association (VEBA), which had a 67.7 percent share, as well as Fiat, which held a 20 percent stake. The United States and Canadian governments counted respective shares of 9.8 and 2.5 percent.

During this period, the last vehicle to emerge from the old Dodge was introduced—the 2009 Dodge Journey crossover. Following this introduction, product programs were frozen as Cerberus and DaimlerChrysler—which up until the bankruptcy still had a 20 percent share in the company—ceded control to Fiat CEO Sergio Marchionne. The new leader proved to be a pivotal leader on the order of Lee Iacocca and Walter Chrysler.

Born in Italy, Marchionne moved with his family to Toronto when he was a teen, giving him dual Italian and Canadian citizenship. He earned degrees in accounting and law in Toronto and Windsor, right across the river from Detroit. Having worked for both accounting firms and multinational corporations, Marchionne was appointed CEO of Fiat S.p.A in 2004, where he engineered a turnaround of the troubled Italian automaker.

A quick student of the global auto industry, Marchionne saw that consolidation was inevitable among the current players. Like Walter Chrysler some 80 years earlier, the Fiat chief saw in the American company the same advantages Chrysler saw in Dodge: state of the art manufacturing and a robust dealer network that meshed neatly with Fiat's operations.

Fiat was strong in Europe and South America, while Chrysler and Dodge had strength in North America. The Jeep brand was also important on two scores—first, it is a true global brand, and second, it has a leadership position in the SUV market, a segment in which Fiat was largely absent.

For Marchionne, it was a perfect fit because Chrysler and Dodge could provide full-size rear-drive sedan platforms sorely needed at Alfa Romeo and Lancia, while Fiat could lend small and mid-size front-drive expertise and fuel efficient engine technology to its new partner. And the tie-up would also pave the way for the company to reintroduce the Fiat and Alfa Romeo brands to America.

Naturally, given the experience of the so-called "marriage of equals" between Daimler-Benz and Chrysler that turned out to be anything but, there was a fair amount of skepticism about the deal in Detroit and among the dealer body. But Marchionne has proven to be a different kind of executive, introducing a leadership style that is based upon meritocracy, embracing competition, aiming for best-in-class performance, and always delivering what is promised.

The 2013 Dodge Dart is based on a widened platform that is used on the Alfa Romeo Giulietta hatchback. The new three-box sedan was developed in just 18 months and is the spiritual successor to the Neon.

The Dodge Grand Caravan
with Blacktop® package.

In a speech to a 2010 national dealer meeting, Marchionne promised "a style of management that doesn't take the approach of 'master of the world,' but rather seeks to establish the ideal conditions for a true sharing of values and knowledge."

And it is also the only way to create an alliance between Chrysler and Fiat that is a partnership in the truest sense. An alliance that fosters growth and creates real value, rather than just inflating numbers."

Marchionne promised, "By 2014, Fiat and Chrysler combined will be able to produce six million vehicles, a critical threshold to be a competitive global player in the auto sector.

"Joining the strengths of the two organizations will enable us to optimize the allocation of capital, fully leverage the potential of the distribution networks, utilize our technological know-how to the fullest, and apply it across the combined product ranges of the two businesses."

"The presence and experience of Fiat in the smaller car segments and of Chrysler in the medium and larger segments will enable the combined groups to offer a full product range and compete in all relevant market segments," he added.

In addition to bringing technology and a new approach to product development, marketing also underwent a profound change. The decision was made to separate the Ram truck brand from Dodge, allowing each to have its own unique designers, engineers, and marketing direction.

Dodge employed a similar strategy for the introduction of the fifth-generation Viper; thus, the new Street & Racing Technology (SRT) brand, originally formed in 2002 as a performance vehicle group, was born in 2012. SRT had existed as primarily an engineering group that developed high-performance vehicles across the Chrysler portfolio, but it was decided to consolidate those efforts and turn SRT into a retail brand with the Viper as its halo car.

Dodge was the first beneficiary of the global expertise of Fiat when work began on the all-new 2013 Dodge Dart. This 4-door, 3-box sedan replaced the crossover-inspired Caliber and became the spiritual successor to the Neon.

Built off a new platform called Compact U.S. Wide (CUSW), the Dart uses a modified version of the architecture that underpins the Alfa Romeo Giulietta hatchback in Italy. The Dart's traditional sedan body style with its wider stance is specifically tailored to American tastes. While most new cars can take three to four years to develop, much of the work on the Dart was completed in 18 months. The all-new Dart was first shown to the public at the 2012 North American International Auto Show in Detroit.

The Dart deftly blends traditional styling cues with cutting-edge engine technology and sporty road manners influenced by the Alfa Romeo lineage. Offered in six trim levels, the Dart features a choice of three different engines—the most fuel-efficient is the innovative 1.4-liter turbocharged 160-horsepower MultiAir 4-cylinder engine developed by Fiat, which can develop up to 41-mile-per-gallon highway mileage in the Aero package. Also offered are 2.0-liter 160-horsepower and 184-horsepower 2.4-liter Tigershark 4-cylinder engines. The Dart also offers three six-speed transmissions in either full automatic, traditional manual, or twin-clutch automated manual with sequential shift.

Pricing starts in the mid-teens, which also earned the Dart recognition by both *Consumer Guide* and *Kelly Blue Book* as one of the "10 Coolest Cars under $18,000."

## A NEW ERA FOR DODGE

The introduction of the Dart is the dawn of a new era at Dodge and provides a fitting cornerstone for a future that will continue to break ground with cutting edge technology without losing sight of the traditional values that have stood the division in good stead for a century.

From the earliest days, Dodge has been and will continue to be a brand that separates itself from the more mainstream. It is a brand that embodies distinctive sporty design, passion, performance, innovation, and technology.

New engines and new technology, such as the 3.6-liter Pentastar V-6 with up to 305 horsepower and the new 8-speed ZF automatic transmission, also mirror the Dodge Brothers commitment to continually upgrade the product. The 2014 Durango embodies this belief by merging strong visual enhancements with a new 8-speed automatic and state-of-the-art electronics, just three years after being engineered all-new from the ground up.

Paying homage to the go-go '60s is the Plum Crazy paint scheme offered on today's Dodge Challenger.

The Charger and Challenger, with their direct links to the Golden Age of the American Muscle Car, continue to offer a nostalgic kick in the pants with thoroughly modern mechanicals at even higher levels of performance. The Charger and Challenger retain their distinct designs that are modern interpretations of the original "fuselage" bodied versions that debuted respectively in 1968 and 1970. Adding to the fun factor is the resurrection of classic colors like Plum Crazy and HEMI Orange as part of the Challenger's color choices.

For 2014, Dodge is celebrating its 100th Anniversary with special editions commemorating this significant milestone on its two most iconic nameplates—the Charger and Challenger. The combination of "100 Years" with the modern-era red hash marks represents a brand that both remembers where it has come from and is ready for the future. The round badge, in particular, pays homage to Dodge's roots, being somewhat historical in itself—long before Dodge established a shield or wings, its logo existed within such a circle.

In every respect, the Anniversary editions of the Charger and Challenger capture the essence of the Dodge brand, which is very much rooted in its machinist heritage, evocative styling, and attention to detail, brought together by a group of designers, engineers, and workers who share a similar passion and respect for this storied brand.

# DODGE 100

In 1914, a total of 146 different auto manufacturers were established in the United States. Only one survives—Dodge.

Dodge celebrates a century.

Today's Dodge is the sum of a car-building legacy that stretches back a century. It's not the same company founded by John and Horace Dodge, but it is still rooted in the basic values laid down by the founders. If the first 50 years were about building a reputation of engineering excellence and dependability, the second 50 have been about infusing the product with passion and performance. Throughout the past century, Dodge has never lost its focus on delivering cutting-edge technology, power, distinctive style, and innovation.

It's a commitment that's paid off. Despite tracing its roots back to the earliest days of the industry, Dodge appeals to a young demographic. The average buyer is 10 years younger than the division's competitive set, and the brand projects an image of passionate, athletic, innovative, and performance-driven vehicles.

And though each vehicle has its own personality, the current lineup projects a part of a much larger identity; indeed, Dodge has its own dedicated design studio staffed with designers who are immersed in the brand. There is a real cohesive look beginning to take shape in the 2014 line of vehicles, including the introduction of the 2013 Dart and the redesigned 2014 Durango. As for the Charger and Challenger, they help set key design cues across the entire line—something not entirely new to Dodge. And even though Ram is now a separate division, Dodge is not abandoning the crosshair in its grilles, but rather building on this signature cue.

The same goes for the racetrack loop rear light assembly, which is a Charger styling cue that has been adapted by both Dart and Durango. Each instance, however, has a specific interpretation relative to the vehicle on which it appears. And although Dodge is one of the Chrysler divisions associated with cab-forward design, there isn't a major overarching philosophy at work on the current lineup; instead, the focus is on the look or attitude of the design to establish a family appearance. Even color plays an important role in defining that attitude, and that's why the wild colors from the muscle-car era, such as Plum Crazy, are making a comeback.

Interior design is just as crucial as the exterior shape. The approach to most of the cars in the Dodge lineup is to stress the driver's side of the cabin. There is room to create an interior that reflects the Dodge attitude, propelling it into the twenty-first century. For example, one interior feature that designers are beginning to take advantage of is the new-generation touchscreens and reconfigurable thin film transistor (TFT) displays in the dash.

## MORE THAN BELLS AND WHISTLES

Dodge is about more than just a sexy shape or enticing interiors. The Dodge brand is tearing into its centennial year with a keen eye focused on the future and a desire to create vehicles customers can't wait to drive and are proud to park in their driveways.

This family portrait shows the full line.

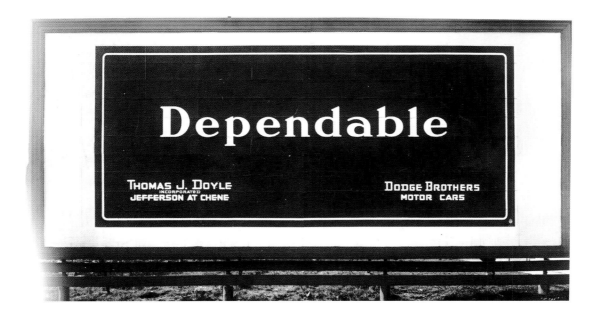

An early billboard sums up the Dodge brand promise: dependable.

With 100 years of history, Dodge is building on the technological advancements of the '30s and '40s, the design evolution of the '50s, the racing heritage of the '60s, the horsepower of the '70s, the efficiency of the '80s, and the unbelievable styling of the '90s as it paves the road to its future.

Dodge continues to build on its performance heritage with its unwavering commitment to no-compromise engines that deliver both power and fuel economy. From its 1.4-liter turbocharged MultiAir 4-cylinder engine up through the HEMI V-8 engines that feature cylinder deactivation, Dodge delivers on that promise. Dodge is also leading the way with cutting-edge eight-speed automatic transmissions.

But it's not just about having great handling or a powerful engine, either; it's also about infusing the product with the latest technologies. As a result, Dodge offers the Uconnect Touchscreen Media Center with 3D maps, downloadable apps, and Wi-Fi hotspots in its cars, as well as dual Blu-ray/DVD entertainment systems, 7-inch TFT customizable gauge clusters, and safety features such as forward collision warning with crash mitigation.

Dodge continues to evolve the Grand Caravan, offering the unique Stow 'n Go system that allows both second- and third-row seats to fold directly into the floor.

Versatility is another Dodge hallmark. It has a 4-door muscle car in the Charger, Stow 'n Go seating in its Grand Caravan, SUV capability with crossover fuel efficiency in the Durango, in-seat and in-floor storage in the 7-passenger Journey, and mid-size roominess in the compact Dodge Dart.

What separates Dodge is that they make all of this style, technology, and versatility approachable. The blend of value and attitude is best shown in the Blacktop appearance package that spreads across the entire lineup. Providing a customized appearance, the Blacktop is part of a philosophy of offering the customer features that make the car stand apart from the mainstream. This same strategy has led to the development of other unique packages, including the Rally, Redline, Daytona, and many more.

The 2014 Dodge lineup includes five vehicles awarded the Insurance Institute for Highway Safety (IIHS) Top Safety Pick title and two named as Top Safety Pick+, five vehicles with best-in-

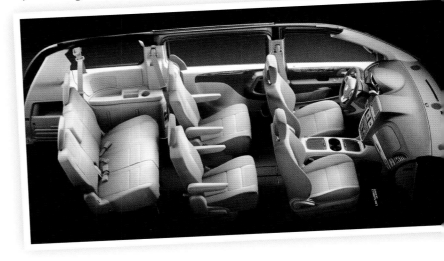

class power, seven vehicles that deliver 25 miles per gallon (mpg) or higher, three vehicles that deliver 31 miles per gallon or higher, and three vehicles that offer seating for seven.

There's no doubt that today's auto industry is a global affair. Global influences are felt both here and in the far corners of the world. To this day, Dodge benefits from that trend, as evidenced by the collaboration with Fiat on the Dart. Still, there are some traits that are uniquely American, and they continue to be embodied in the products wearing the Dodge nameplate. These timeless characteristics are honesty, authenticity, utility, great design, driving enjoyment, and value.

Although the ram is no longer the official mascot, there is much to be said about the imagery of this animal—surefooted, persistent, and tough, the ram is a fighter. And the ram spirit lives on in Dodge to this day.

The story of the Dodge brothers and the car company they founded is the story of America. Dodge has survived ownership changes, bailouts, and bankruptcy. It has a proud heritage of serving the military in war and providing affordable transportation for all in peace. Dodge has stood by America for 100 years, and the country, in turn, has stood by Dodge.

Dodge's proud history and bold legacy promises to continue for a long time. Its past and its future are best summed up by a 1972 ad campaign that echoes a recurring theme:

Dodge. Depend on it.

Left, top: Brampton, Ontario, is a long way from Dodge Main both in time and geography. Although both used moving assembly lines, the modern plant is cleaner and builds cars with greater precision.

Left, bottom: The Durango grille shows how the crosshair design theme continues to be refined with a wider center.

Below: The Dodge Dart GT is the newst member of the lineup and emodies the division's youthful, sporty image.

The Dodge 100th Anniversary
Edition Charger and Challenger.

# INDEX